# FENG SHUI FIX IT!

# FENG SHUI FIX IT!

## 100 Solutions for a Happier Home

CLIFF TAN

BATSFORD

Contents

## Furniture arrangement and placement



## Compass and superstition



## Furniture, lights and fixtures

## Colours



## Storage and clutter



## Outside the home



## General

# Introduction

Let me share a little story. Many years ago, when I was a small boy, my friend hosted a sleepover. I was late, so by the time I arrived everyone had placed their sleeping bags around the room, and the only spot left was directly in front of the door. I cried and refused to sleep there. Eventually I came up with my own solution, squeezing between two of my friends, leaving that spot in front of the door empty. Everyone thought I was crazy and, in hindsight, maybe I was! As a child, I was told that bad things would happen if I ever slept with my feet pointing to the door. I didn't understand why, but it sounded like scary magic and I was too fearful to go against it.

Fast forward and I now know that this rule came from feng shui, which is the belief that by altering your environment, you can shape your fortunes and your destiny. Feng shui is an ancient practice that originated in China about 3,000 years ago as a guide on where and how to build homes and cities. This knowledge has been passed down generations, and evolved from building towns and forts to the placement of beds and desks.

Like many age-old beliefs with limited scientific evidence, this generational knowledge can be met with scepticism. In fact, many people now regard feng shui as an inconvenient superstition meant to scare you into silly fear-induced obsessions – like me in my friend's house. I don't blame them. It is easy to see how your life's destiny being connected to moving furniture around your home can sound mystical. And it is... in a way. However, there is a logic behind it and reasons for each feng shui rule, so trust me when I say that moving furniture around can actually change your life – as long as you understand the how and why (if you don't believe me, try it and see).

# What is feng shui?

Feng shui is the belief that your physical environment can affect your fortunes. Simply put, it is the practice of setting your spaces up so you can feel good and thrive, working with the energy and elements around you, your home and your environment, connecting how you feel there with how you behave and perform.

To give an example: imagine you're looking for a quiet spot so you can read a book. We have two rooms for you to choose from. One is spacious, bright and quiet, with an open view of a soothing meadow. The other room is smaller, darker, full of people talking; it smells of food and has a tiny window to a brick wall. Of course, the first room feels nicer and would allow you to concentrate, and feng shui would say, choose that room. But that's not feng shui, you might argue, it's just common sense. Indeed, much of feng shui is common sense and practical reasoning. With its millennia of history, feng shui has developed a compendium of knowledge that touches upon almost every aspect of space and environment, even the ones we take for granted.

That said, the two rooms is just a simple example and there are many other rules in feng shui which might not seem quite so logical as picking the room with the best environment for your reading. And that is why, in this book, we're going to address the most common adages associated with feng shui and look at the things that make it sound superstitious head on. We will delve into these beliefs and explain what they mean and why, as well as how to fix them.

# A crash course

Before we get too deep into this, allow me to give you a tiny crash course in the pillars of feng shui. As I have explained, feng shui is about creating the best possible environment for you to thrive in.

To do this, the space around you needs to fulfil a few criteria. The first is that you need to feel safe. In feng shui, this is covered by the concept of the command position, which means placing yourself in the optimal position in any room: positioning yourself so that your back, where you cannot see, is solid and supported, and ahead of you, where you can see, is a nice open view. You can notice what's happening around you, while not feeling too exposed.

The second criteria is to feel nice, and this is where the concept of energy or chi comes in. In feng shui, we are surrounded by forces in the form of light, sound or even memory. These are collectively seen as energy, which affects the way we perceive space. For example, a window with beautiful views is sheng chi, or life energy, while an empty, dark room with cobwebs is si chi, or dead energy. Energy can also come from physical objects. A sharp knife pointing at you is considered sha chi, which is known as killing energy because it makes you feel uneasy. A long fast road angled at you is considered sha chi too, not because it will poke you like a knife, but because it gives off the same kind of uneasy energy.

With all these ideas, feng shui is a sophisticated system on how to calibrate and calculate the energy of space around you. It taps into the concept of yin and yang, which translates to darkness and light, or, more specifically, how energy can be perceived as stronger or weaker based on comparison. Developing on this, we then have the concept of the five elements, where directions, seasons and even time each have qualities determined by how yin and yang they are compared to one another. These are then mapped out on the bagua, tying it all back together.

I know this might start to sound overwhelming, but don't worry, feng shui never expects anyone to learn its logic, but rather to heed its advice, because once you do, your space will be comfortable and you will thrive as a result. But, you might ask, what if you don't? Will bad things start to happen?

# Age-old beliefs

Among the rules that you might consider superstitious are 'never sleep with your head against your bathroom wall' or 'never have a straight path leading to your front door'. Other very specific rules include avoiding decorating your home with antique mirrors or that you should never paint your kitchen dark blue.

And these rules are not just rules: in feng shui, they often come with scary consequences attached. If you were raised with feng shui, you (like me) would know that sleeping with your feet to the door will lead to bad fortune, illness and even death energy, and if your bedroom door faces your sibling's, you will always be arguing. Yes, I know, very dramatic. In fact, these consequences are so specific and particular that it becomes impossible to ignore them. Returning to the bed against a bathroom wall. In feng shui, it is said that if you ignore this rule, the consequence is not just bad – it will actually make you ill, and specifically you will get joint aches and colds. These consequences are so rooted in feng shui that many people raised in this environment subconsciously live by these rules.

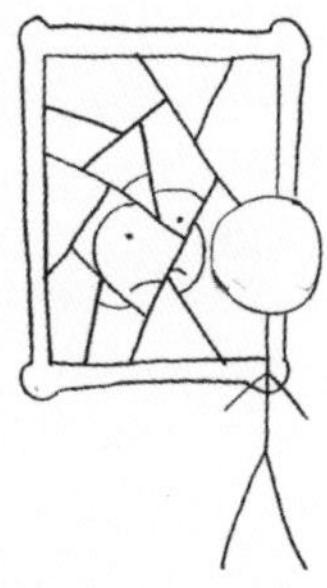

As scary as these may sound, we must remember that feng shui is meant to improve lives – and these consequences were used to convince people who would otherwise not listen to its advice. Remember, thousands of years ago, life was different. People were focused more on survival and necessity than wellbeing. They needed to know that they had to avoid sleeping in such and such a way, hence all those easy-to-remember terrifying consequences.

Of course, now we realise that we won't actually die if we sleep with our feet to the door. But despite how rational we can be, it's natural to feel nervous when you break a rule, and wonder if the reason you have a cold is because you moved your bed to share a wall with the bathroom, or if it was simply a coincidence.

# Fix it!

No home is perfect, and it is important to know that you can make your home work better for you. There may be problems or things that cause little inconveniences or frustration – and you might not even notice it. Your bed might share a wall with the bathroom, and your housemate flushes the toilet in the middle of the night and wakes you up. It's only a small issue, yes, but if you move your bed around, this minor change would make your sleep so much better. Or perhaps it's more than an inconvenience – maybe your mum has just told you that the house you recently purchased has a deadly poison arrow pointing towards it, and as much as you love your home, you somehow cannot help but wonder if your recent accident at work was related to it. Actually knowing what this lore means and how best to suppress its 'powers' could give you priceless peace of mind.

Instead of just living with it – be it an actual daily frustration that annoys you physically or mentally, or the unshakeable idea that inevitable bad fortune will befall you – we are here to fix things once and for all. Fixing something is often easier than we make it out to be, and applying a small effort, even an annoying one, will give you a lifetime of peace and finally put your uncertainties to rest.

So, let's fix it!

# How to use this book

This book contains a hundred well-known feng shui faux pas, arranged by categories.

Each of these faux pas is accompanied by **a rating** on how serious it is, the **superstitious consequence** of each broken rule and **the explanation** of why it's actually a problem and then, most importantly: **the fix**.

# Ratings

Each of these feng shui points is accompanied by a rating on how serious it is.

- 3 frowns: the most serious. Breaking this rule could actually affect your life, not in a strange cursed way, but in ways that you will truly feel. This might affect your mood, your behaviour and your life, and should be taken seriously.

- 2 frowns: moderate. Breaking this rule may make you feel uneasy, especially if you are sensitive to your surroundings. The effect is noticeable but manageable, and you could get used to it over time.

- 1 frown: minor. Most people wouldn't even notice it as a problem. It is good to know, but nothing to worry about.

## Superstitions and explanations

Each broken rule has a superstitious consequence. Now be prepared, these might sound scary and even far-fetched, but this is deliberate. Historically, these warnings were meant to convince people to follow the rules. These consequences are a mix of traditional beliefs and modern interpretations based on energy. Bear in mind though, these interpretations are exaggerated, and less important than the practical explanations that follow.

The explanation is the most important: they help you understand why these problems are problems and how they can actually affect you. Knowledge is power, and I want you to truly understand the root and logic behind each rule so that you can decide if it is something that is relevant to your situation and if the suggested fixes apply to you.

## The fixes!

Finally, we have the fixes, which are suggestions on how you can make things better, from easy fixes that you can try right away to bigger changes that can transform the way your space feels. These are not exhaustive, so with this newfound knowledge, feel free to improvise your own fixes along the way.

# HOME-LAYOUT

# ISSUES

1

# I have stairs just inside my front door

**Rating:**

Feng shui says... if you have stairs directly inside your front door, any wealth that enters your life will not settle but instead disperse.

**Why**

The door is the mouth of your home and any wealth and opportunities come through it, whereas a staircase is like a funnel drawing energy towards it and upwards. Metaphorically, this means that nice energy entering through your door will never make it into your living room, but rather go up the stairs, dissipating into your hallways (especially if the stairs point towards the door).

The reason behind this superstition is that people who enter your house might feel confused and be drawn up the stairs to the private rooms rather than to the living spaces. There are exceptions of course, like if your living spaces are indeed upstairs and you want your guests to head up, or if your entry hallway is large and grand enough that the stairs are not right in your face.

**Fix it!**

Ensure that anyone who enters your home is not confused by the stairs and knows exactly where to go. The advice comes down to this: the prettier your hallway, the less impactful the stairs will be.

- Add a buffer, such as a round rug between the stairs and the door, which will create a transition point before the stairs start.
- Distract the eye. Hang a crystal pendant between the door and stairs so when you enter the room, you look up rather than at the stairs.
- Enhance the entry by hanging art or mirrors (not facing the door) to further create visual distractions from the stairs.
- Guide the eye towards the main living spaces. You can do this by decorating the living area attractively, with beautiful artwork or pendant lights, as well as painting the room a lighter colour than the entryway.

2

# My front door opens straight to my back door, is that bad?

**Rating:**

Feng shui says... if your front door shoots directly out the back door, all the money you earn will be spent just as quickly.

**Why**

Opportunities and fortune enter your life through the front door. When this door is directly aligned with a back door or large window, the home feels like a tunnel. Energy enters, does not settle, and immediately exits. For a home to bear good fortune, it needs to be more like a container, and have a place for this fortune to 'land' or place itself. On a more practical level, this layout makes the home feel exposed and unprotected, with little visual or psychological shelter. Interestingly, this alignment is acceptable in holiday homes, because our focus there is escape.

**Fix it!**

Create visual substance and a sense of containment, so when you enter the home, you focus on the inside.

- Design an entry moment. The front door should, ideally, open into a foyer or transitional space. Even if the view is really nice, save it for a gradual reveal.
- Block the direct line by hanging curtains to cover the window or door, breaking the energetic flow.
- Add plants along the window to obscure and soften the view. This way you still maintain the views out the window.
- Draw your attention into the home. Furnish the interior nicely so that you feel invited in, not pulled out.
- Hang crystals between the front door and back door. These will absorb the energy. Practically, a nice pendant light will draw your attention upwards and not through.
- Interrupt the pathway by placing furniture like armchairs between the doors.

3

# My entrance opens into my living room

*(the postman sees me in my pyjamas)*

**Rating:**

Feng shui says... when your front door opens directly into your private space, you will feel unstable and be easily disturbed.

### Why

Your front door opening directly into your living room means that you welcome anyone into your life and home. While this is friendly and nice, it also means that you are unprepared for those who you might not want inside. In ancient Chinese homes, there was always a screen inside the front door, called a spirit gate, to filter and prevent unwanted spirits from entering homes and lives without a proper transition. Practically, an open layout means that if your door is left open, your neighbours could easily peek into your home and see you in your underwear every time they walk past.

### Fix it!

Block out as much of the view into your private space as possible.

- Place a screen or build a feature wall directly in front of the door which works to create a foyer space. But be aware of how this screen redirects you. If it forces you towards the kitchen, that's even worse, so this may not always be the solution.
- Redirect attention away from the living space. Create a pretty corner that draws the eye, which would work nicely with the money corner (see page 106), since it is also usually in view of the door.
- Avoid being in the open. Take note of where you spend the most time in the living space – like your couch – and place it on the more protected side of the room so you are always out of view.
- Change the direction of the door. Sometimes the solution may be as simple as changing the way the door swings, so the flow of energy is diverted away from the private zone.

4

# The kitchen is the first thing I see when I come home, it's so chaotic

**Rating:** 

Feng shui says... if you see the stove the moment you enter your home, all your wealth will burn away.

**Why**

A kitchen usually contains a stove where food is, traditionally, thrown into a fire (although hobs might be more common now). Although food is seen as abundance, a kitchen is an aggressive space that is often chaotic and messy. The front door, on the other hand, is where fortune rings in, and where your guests come in with opportunities. So it is important for this positive energy to settle nicely and not be immediately consumed by fire. Even if you don't have guests, entering an unorganised kitchen is not welcoming for you either. You are immediately confronted with tasks, which creates a sense of tension. Over time, you might start to associate coming home with being cooked alive.

**Fix it!**

Reduce this chaotic energy as much as possible and create a welcoming feel. Avoid seeing the stove or the sink from the front door! The stove represents your wealth burning away, while the sink represents your wealth draining out. Kitchen counters are less intense, as long as they look tidy.

- Redirect attention away from the kitchen with consoles or a well-organised shoe cabinet.
- Keep the kitchen as tidy as possible. Use closed cabinetry and plain-looking containers to reduce visual clutter. This applies to open-plan kitchens as well.
- Add things that represent abundance or create beauty. Place a large and colourful bowl of fruit right in the middle of the counter so it is the first thing you notice, rather than the messy sink. This is particularly important if your kitchen is located in the money corner of your home.
- Use cohesive colours and finishes. If you are designing or renovating your kitchen, choose colours that complement those in the living areas so it does not stand out on its own.
- Draw the eye upward. Since the mess is usually on the counter, hang pretty pendant lights or crystals to draw attention upwards.

5

# My front door faces the toilet, I can't use it when guests are coming

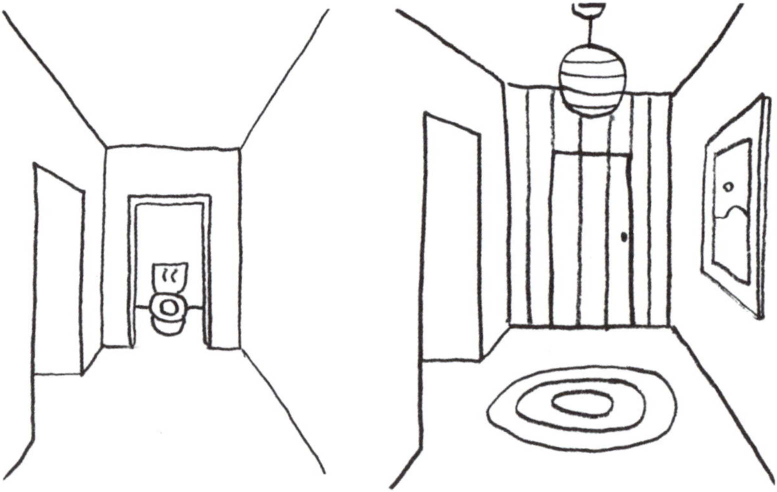

**Rating:**

Feng shui says... if your front door faces your toilet, all your wealth will be flushed away.

### Why

A toilet is designed to flush out smelly waste. It's a big hole that sucks all the bad things away and is essentially a portal out of our home and our lives. The front door is the main way into our homes, which means all the good fortune and wealth enter through it. Put these two elements in one straight line and you can see why it's said that having your front door facing the toilet means that all the wealth and fortune that should have been coming your way are just as quickly flushed away. Practically, a toilet is simply unpleasant to look at and can create embarrassment when guests arrive, which may also subtly affect how confident you feel, gradually influencing how you value your own space.

### Fix it!

Avoid seeing the toilet by either hiding it or creating visual distractions.

- The best solution is to avoid direct alignment. If you are renovating or building, design your entrance so that the toilet is not the first thing you see. Even changing the way the door swings can help. As long as you don't see the toilet, its physical proximity to the door is less of an issue.
- Camouflage the door. Use doors that match with the colours or textures of the walls, so it is less noticeable.
- Hide the toilet bowl. If the placement of the bathroom is unavoidable, position the toilet so it is not the first thing you see when you enter.
- Visually distract the eye. Make the bathroom attractive with art, knick-knacks and plants. If something beautiful catches your attention, the toilet will be less dominant.
- Keep the toilet lid closed at all times, as that will reduce its draining effect.
- Hang a crystal or chandelier in the hallway to distract the eye and send good energy upwards and away from the bathroom and back into the home.

6

# I only ever enter through my garage door because it's easier

**Rating:** 

Feng shui says... an unused front door means rewards and recognition will never come.

### Why

In feng shui, wealth and personal energy come together, so wealth enters your home the same way you do. If you enter your home by the back door, garage or laundry, wealth will still follow you in, but if your rear entrance is unwelcoming – say it's a messy, cramped boot room – you might start to feel like you're sneaking in, an intruder in your own home. This subtle feeling extends to prosperity. Fortune and other happy energies will feel rejected, almost as if your home does not deserve them. In the long run, this ritual will eventually crush your confidence and satisfaction in your home, which affects how you feel in life.

### Fix it!

Make whichever entrance you use feel nicer and more welcoming.

- Keep it tidy. Even if you are entering through the laundry room, it should not feel like a laundry. Ensure that there is enough storage (with doors) to contain utility items, and leave space at the entrance to drop off things so they stay clear of the floor – like a coat rack or a shoe cabinet. Store occasionally used items elsewhere (that coat you wear twice a year) so the entrance remains functional and uncluttered.
- Add touches of beauty, such as artwork or plants (make sure they're alive, see page 158). These may seem superfluous, but they offer the priceless feeling of confidence and ownership.
- Enhance the outside. The exterior journey to the door should be pleasant too, even if it's at the rear of the house. Try to create a clear and pretty pathway to whichever entrance you want to use, so that it feels intentional and welcoming.
- Ensure the door can open freely without resistance, so no piles of coats forcing you to squeeze your way in.
- Use your front door! Don't reserve it only for important guests. The most important person to enter your home is you.

7

# My entry hallway is long and narrow, it's so depressing

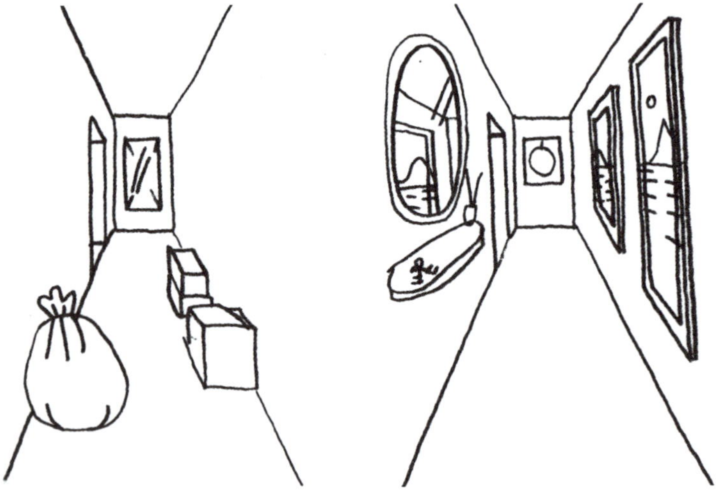

**Rating:** 

Feng shui says... a narrow entrance hallway creates a rush of energy, which may cause health problems.

### Why

Your entrance is the mouth of your home where chi flows in. Therefore it is important that it feels welcoming and generous, ready to receive good energy and to let the prosperity linger. Practically, when your entrance is too narrow, you have no place to put down your things and you are forced through, making you feel restricted, rushed and stifled. This subconsciously causes dissatisfaction with your home and in your life. While you might argue that this is only a small part of the home, this first impression is lasting and significant.

### Fix it!

Make the entrance feel as open and welcoming as possible, despite its physical dimensions.

- Add utility-like shelves or drop-off zones. Even if the hallway is tight, it needs to be useful. That could just mean adding a little shelf for your keys – do it!
- Keep it tidy. Avoid clutter such as recycling in the hallway and store shoes in closed storage, ideally at waist height or lower so it does not close the space.
- Use art. Hang large artwork of landscapes or open views, as these behave like windows and take your attention off the big blank walls, making the hallway feel less claustrophobic.
- Use mirrors strategically. Mirrors can double the perceived width of a space, but avoid reflecting inauspicious things like your bathroom or kitchen. Never hang a mirror at the end of the hallway, as that will make it look even narrower.
- Use lighting to add depth to the space. Either use spotlights to focus on the artwork, wall lights to create instances of light and depth along the wall, or diffused cove lighting to create softness and calm. Avoid single ceiling lights, as these flatten the space and cast harsh shadows.

8

# The toilet is right in the centre of my home, it's so smelly all the time

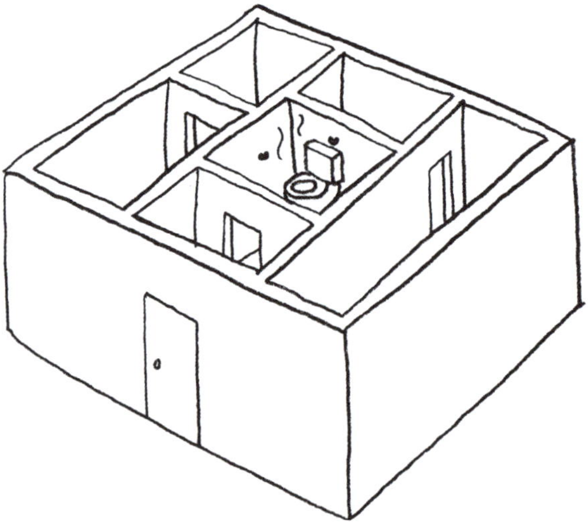

**Rating:** 

Feng shui says... a toilet in the middle of your home will make you feel ill, especially in the stomach.

**Why**

Picture this: you're living in a house in ancient China around 3,000 years ago. There is no plumbing or sanitation, and the toilet is nothing more than an outhouse in your garden. It's smelly, it's unpleasant, and you want it to be as far from the house as practically possible. Placing your toilet inside the home, particularly in the heart of it, would have caused contamination and illnesses. Fast forward to today. Even though modern bathrooms have ventilation systems and good plumbing to take the waste away, the toilet is still seen as an unpleasant place full of bacteria. We don't want to be constantly reminded of it, and we definitely don't want to see it when we are eating or watching TV.

**Fix it!**

Ideally, plan your home so that the toilet isn't in the middle of the home, but if it has to be, try to make it as discreet as possible.

- Hide the toilet from view so you can forget it exists. Use hidden doors or – at the very least! – paint the door the same colour as the walls. If there is enough space, use a screen to hide the door.
- A slightly indirect route to the toilet will make it feel less like it's in the heart of the home, so redirect the toilet entrance if you can!
- If you can change your bathroom, separate the toilet from the sink area. Within the bathroom, position the sink and vanity first, with the toilet tucked behind a partition or low wall. This creates a barrier and keeps the toilet out of immediate view.
- Always keep the toilet doors closed and hidden. This applies to toilets next to living areas and dining rooms as well.
- Make the bathroom a pleasant place. If it cannot be hidden from view, at least make it look pretty, with nice artwork and scents – and keep it clean.

9

# The toilet is above my bedroom

**Rating:** 

Feng shui says... having a toilet above you when you sleep will cause you to become ill over time.

**Why**

Toilets symbolise waste and unwanted things, which you get rid of and flush away as soon as you can. Imagine having to sleep under a toilet, where the only thing between you and your housemate's poop is a flimsy PVC pipe. Even if your pipes are well built, just knowing there is actively flowing sewage above can cause uncontrollable unease. In fact, in feng shui we try to avoid having not just bedrooms, but other important spaces such as dining rooms, living rooms and especially kitchens under bathrooms and toilets. Superstitions aside, your senses can subconsciously pick up on the toilet cues, such as visible pipes, the sounds of flushing, movement of water, or even the awareness of waste above and potential of leakage. All these can make you feel less safe, affecting your ability to rest.

**Fix it!**

Ideally avoid having a bed under a toilet, but if it's not possible, the goal is to increase distance and protection.

- Move your bed. The key parts are your face and the toilet pipes. Try to shift so that your head and pillow are not directly under the toilet. Picture the toilet leaking: you just don't want its liquid to be dripping onto your nose.

- Add a buffer. You can either create a false ceiling or use a canopy bed with ample fabric draping over it so that there is a shield between you, your ceiling and the floor of the toilet. This is especially important if the pipes are visible (box the pipes up!).

- Warm up your room. Waste from toilets is associated with water, so use warm colours and ambient lights to make your room feel cosy and dry, keeping the wet toilet energy at bay.

- Hang a visually powerful object like a pendant light to 'catch' the toilet flow above. This is especially useful for other rooms like entrances and living spaces.

10

# My bedroom is over the kitchen and I can smell food

**Rating:** 

Feng shui says... sleeping over a stove will make you angry and hot tempered.

### Why

A kitchen is an active, hot place full of energy and fire. Imagine that 3,000 years ago a kitchen would literally have had open flames and smoke. Not only is that dangerous, but the high bustle and energy of a kitchen is intensely yang, at odds with the peaceful yin nature of a bedroom, which will disrupt sleep. Of course, now kitchens are not as violent as they once were, with extraction systems and more subdued electric or induction alternatives for stoves, but the awareness that someone could be boiling a wok of hot oil right under your bed on what's supposed to be a peaceful Sunday morning sleep-in is still there. This also applies to rooms beside and under kitchens. While fire technically only spreads up, even a room under a kitchen would feel the activity and energy above it, and so it's best to sleep as far from a kitchen as possible.

### Fix it!

Avoid using the rooms over kitchens as bedrooms, but if it's unavoidable, the trick is to create separation, insulation and a sense of cool.

- Avoid the stove itself. If your bedroom is over a kitchen, the first thing you should do is position your bed so that no part of it is over the stove or oven.
- Add insulation, especially if your head is over the stove and you can't move your bed. Add a thick rug under your bed and choose a colour which is earthy or cool to 'soak' up the fire raging beneath.
- Block or redirect the smoke and fire in the kitchen. Be sure to use a very good extractor fan to ensure no smoke or smells can penetrate the floorboards, so that you are not reminded of the cooking happening below.
- Reduce the fire itself. Use electric or induction cooktops instead of a gas fire, and restrict stovetop cooking to non-sleeping hours.
- Limit connection. If you share a wall with a kitchen, don't place your bed against the same wall as the stove or, if you have to, then add a thick, sturdy headboard.

11

# My stove is so close to my sink

**Rating:** 😐

Feng shui says... stoves and sinks next to each other represent a clash of elements that will cause disagreements and arguments.

**Why**

Stoves represent the upward-rising fire element – burning, fuelling, creating – while sinks represent the downward-flowing water element – fluid, cold, cleansing. While each has their own merits, if placed too close to each other they not only cancel each other out, but create a sense of imbalance and disharmony. Think of hot cooking oil and water: they are stable on their own, but when you put them together, they fight and splatter. Placing your stove too close to your sink is not only visually awkward, but makes each of them more physically difficult to use. Imagine one person cooking while the other is doing the dishes; you will be constantly in each other's way. It could also be dangerous, with the splash of washing vegetables just inches away from a cauldron of boiling oil.

**Fix it!**

Create distance between the stove and sink, both physically and mentally.

- Leave a minimum distance of 2ft or 60cm between them, enough space so that it's useable. If that means using a smaller stove or sink, do it.
- Stagger them. If they are opposite each other – for example, your stove is on a kitchen island – be sure they are not directly opposite each other. If you can't stagger them, introduce a rug. Choose green to represent the wood element, or browns to represent the earth element.
- Add a buffer between them, such as a little plant or herb, which is an element of wood. This will act like a leafy screen blocking your washing liquid from splashing into your stove.
- Emphasise the fire element, which will minimise the tension. Do this by making the stove stand out more by using a backsplash with warm, reddish tones.

12

# My kids' bedroom doors face each other and it feels intense

**Rating:**

Feng shui says… if the doors of your children's rooms face each other, they will argue and fight.

**Why**

Facing doors can be confrontational. Imagine that every time you exit your room, you are faced with your brother or sister's door: you will uncontrollably and unnecessarily think of them – along with all their associations. This repeated visual reminder will keep that person always on your mind, amplifying any existing feelings of irritation, challenge and comparison. This isn't limited to siblings; it applies to neighbours and housemates too. If the relationship is already warm and friendly, this might actually strengthen the connection. The idea of conflict comes from the assumption that siblings are more likely to be in competition, and therefore facing doors is best avoided.

**Fix it!**

If the doors cannot be moved, the key is to break the direct line of sight between them.

- Hang a door curtain, like a noren (a traditional Japanese curtain with a cut in the middle), on one or both of the doors. This ensures that even if the doors are opened, there will be no line of sight through them.
- Camouflage the doors by painting them the same colour as the walls, to make them visually more subtle.
- Add a buffer near the doors, such as a piece of furniture like a console or plant.
- Redirect attention from the doors by hanging art on the wall near them or at the end of the corridor.
- As a last resort, hang a crystal between the doors. This will draw the attention and deflect the energy between them. But make sure no one will hit their head!
- Do not hang a bagua mirror facing your neighbour's door, as this is an unfriendly gesture.

13

# My bedroom is over the garage, it feels so unstable

**Rating:** 

Feng shui says… if your room is over a garage, you will become emotionally disconnected and feel unstable.

**Why**

A garage is not considered a 'real' space. It contains no living people and has no meaningful uses, and is seen as unnourished and transitional. Having a bedroom over it is like your room being balanced atop tiny stilts over a restless, rushing river. This, of course, makes the room feel unsupported and detached. With its lack of proper structure or foundation, the room is more like an annexe, and would subconsciously make anyone living there feel excluded from the main home. On a more practical note, a garage is usually built using different materials or methods than the house and is often left uninsulated. This means temperature fluctuations and sound disturbances could be felt by the room above, causing discomfort. This applies to rooms over porches as well.

**Fix it!**

If you can't avoid living spaces above the garage, try to make the space feel more secure and sound.

- Avoid having the master bedroom over the garage. The owners of the home should always sleep within the main body of the house. Try to repurpose it as a spare room or office instead.
- Insulate and protect the room. Add insulation in the ceiling of the garage to ensure that the temperature is constant and controlled, which will also keep the noise or resonance of rolling doors to a minimum.
- Strengthen the base of the room. Do this by keeping the garage clean, tidy and orderly, and always secure and closed. A closed garage is better than an open car port.
- Keep the room warm and cosy to give a grounding effect. Do this by having thick, earthy rugs under your bed, and decorating the room so it feels embracing and snug.
- Make the garage look like it's part of the home. Externally, use the same materials so the garage and room above it feel like they are one with the main house.

14

# My room is L-shaped and it's so hard to arrange

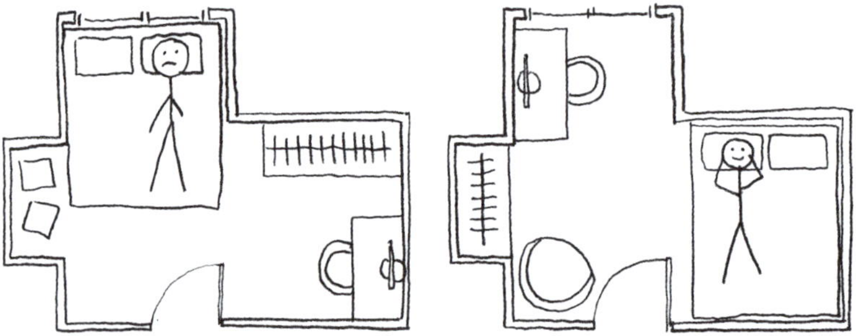

**Rating:** 

Feng shui says... a room with missing corners or extra protrusions means your life will feel incomplete.

**Why**

Oddly shaped rooms – 'L' shaped, triangular or trapezoidal – are not just tricky to furnish, but create unbalanced energy. In feng shui, missing sections in a room symbolise missing parts of our lives. We like to have a clear overview of our lives and environment before making plans. So when parts of the room are missing or hidden, it translates to uncertainty or compromise. Practically, irregular rooms often have areas that are more exposed and busier, while other parts might feel unusable or dead. This can make us feel squeezed in some areas, but like we're wasting something in others, which can lead to feelings of frustration or inward tension.

**Fix it!**

How bad a room feels depends on just how funny its shape is, but the aim is to try to make it feel complete.

- Identify key energy zones. Open areas tend to have higher energy, and tucked-away corners will carry lower energy. Identify each and zone out your room based on this.
- Use low-energy corners for supporting activities. Small corners can be used for storage which, if done nicely, can look flush to the other walls and 'complete' the shape of your room. Larger corners can become cosy sleeping nooks, especially if your focus is on space rather than relationships.
- Reserve higher-energy areas for your desk or couch areas, which are your 'main' activities. These spaces should be left as open as you can.
- Soften angles and sharp corners. If your room is angled or trapezoidal, place plants or furniture in these areas to soften the sharp corners. Use circular rugs to de-emphasise the angled walls.
- Expand tight corners by using lights, mirrors or artwork (depending on the room's function) to make them feel more spacious.

# ARCHITECTURAL

# ELEMENTS

15

# My bedroom is in the attic and has sloped ceilings

**Rating:**

Feng shui says… a big sloping roof can cause headaches and stifled progress in life.

**Why**

A sloping ceiling is seen as inauspicious in feng shui because ceilings represent the sky, and one that slopes can make it feel like the sky is falling or 'pushing down' on you, so you feel trapped or weighed down. The practical reasoning is, of course, that you might find yourself hitting your head on the ceiling, and so over time you'll naturally hunch and restrict yourself, which will translate to your life! This does depend on just how low the ceiling comes down. If the space is high enough that even at the lowest points of the ceiling you can stand up straight, then it will cause no issues.

**Fix it!**

While we cannot change the shape of the ceiling, we can place furniture in a way that reduces the feeling of being pressed down.

- Place the bed in the part of the room with a higher ceiling. However, if this creates an awkward layout, place the bed at the lowest point of the ceiling – as long as you can sit up in bed without hitting your head.
- Fill in the space. If the slope comes down too low and you can't sit up in bed, pull it out from the wall until you can sit up and fill the gap between the bed and wall with storage to create a buffer zone. If the storage behind is hard to access, use it for items you only use occasionally.
- Put storage furniture at the lowest parts of the room. Adding low cabinets or shelves not only offers more storage, but also prevents you from walking too far into the slope and hitting your head.
- Visually soften the ceiling's presence. Paint the ceiling and walls the same colour to blur the boundary, and use indirect lighting like table lamps to 'push' the ceiling up, creating a visual depth that makes the room feel less oppressive.
- For desks, always avoid sitting facing the low point of the ceiling; sit perpendicular to the slope or with the slope behind you. If there is no other place for your desk, make sure it is very deep to keep you away from the slope. Use a large computer screen to symbolise openness.

16

# There's a beam over my head when I sleep and it feels so heavy

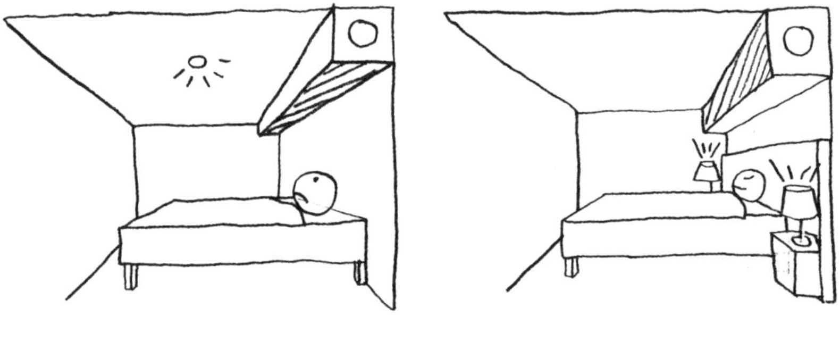

**Rating:** 

Feng shui says... having a beam over your bed will give you headaches and migraines.

**Why**

A beam is a heavy structural element, supporting not just your ceiling, but sometimes an entire building full of other apartments. Sleeping under one will put your body in a constant state of subtle pressure. This is because your subconscious registers it as something pressing down on you. Over time, this can lead to uneasy and disrupted sleep. This also applies to pipe boxing that hides ventilation shafts or pipes. Depending on the design, coved ceilings can cause a similar problem. They all create an oppressive weight over your head, which symbolically weighs down on your thoughts.

**Fix it!**

Reduce the visual weight of beams and make them blend into the walls.

- Paint the beam or boxing in the same colour as the walls and ceilings to visually blend them together.
- Avoid creating new pipe boxing. Try to direct pipes in other ways and not over the bed, or build the boxing as small as possible.
- Avoid ceiling designs that create beams, for example coved/dropped ceilings, or ceiling lightboxes.
- Use a tall, solid headboard. This will give the impression of a strong wall behind the bed, mentally supporting you against the weight above.
- Use side lighting. Have nightstands with table lights shining upwards, which will essentially 'push' the structures up and away from you.
- Use hidden integrated lighting such as LED strips along the headboard for a soft ambient light that de-emphasises the ceiling.
- Consider a four-poster bed, especially with a canopy, as it will protect the bed from any visual weight overhead.

# There's a beam that cuts through my room, can I sleep or sit under it?

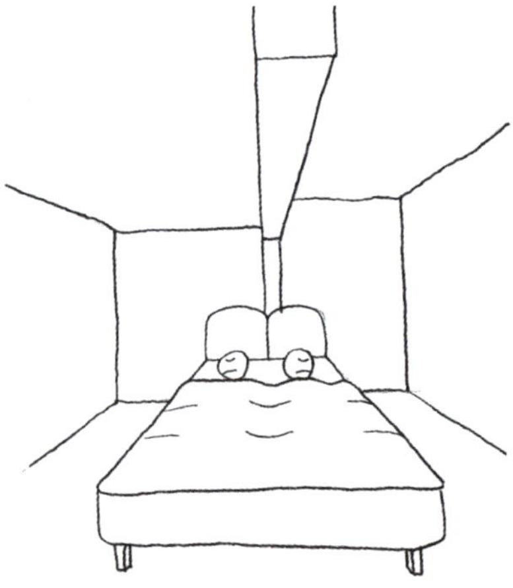

**Rating:** 

Feng shui says... if a couple sleeps under a beam that cuts down the middle of their bed, they will split up.

### Why

A beam is a structural element that holds the roof up. When there is a beam in the middle of a room, it typically signifies a separate structural section. If two people are sleeping on either side of it, they feel as though they are on separate sides of the home. Even if this is not structurally true, beams visually divide space, like a blade suspended over you. Placing something that symbolises togetherness, such as a bed or couch, under a beam like this creates a symbolic division, with the space telling you that you are not fully sharing the same zone. Besides looking strange, being under a beam also gives a feeling of pressure and tension, which is uncomfortable. This applies to other rooms as well, such as living and dining rooms, where placing your couch or table under a beam represents a similar split.

### Fix it!

Remove the visual and psychological weight of the beam as much as possible.

- Hide the beam completely. Building a false ceiling to make the entire room feel like one space is the best option, even if the ceiling has to be lowered.
- Paint the beam(s) and ceiling the same colour. This helps to blend everything together. Do not emphasise them with contrasting colours.
- Try not to place furniture directly under a beam. Arrange your furniture so that beds or seating areas are on one side of it.
- Avoid overhead lighting, as this creates shadows that emphasise the presence of a beam. Use indirect lighting to bring the eye downwards and leave the ceiling in shadow.
- Hang large artworks on the wall under the beam to bridge the divide and draw your attention away from the ceiling.

# The air-conditioner is above my head, I'm freezing

**Rating:** 

Feng shui says... sleeping under an air-conditioner can weaken your health over time.

### Why

This may be one of the more practical feng shui concerns. Sleeping under an air-conditioner has obvious consequences. It is a huge machine that constantly blows cold air right onto your face and, in some instances, drips condensation down your wall as you lie in deep sleep, unaware. Your body will be working hard to regulate your temperature, and your face, being the only part of your body that is left exposed, will bear the brunt of the breeze. Even if you don't actually have cold air funnelling down your nose, the presence of a huge machine whirling all night may cause subconscious stress, either through the sounds that it makes or the way it looks, looming above you.

### Fix it!

Avoid placing your head directly under the AC, or try to direct the air away from you.

- Limit night-time operation. Either turn it off during sleep times, or turn it to its lowest setting.
- Redirect airflow by using an air deflector or cassette to push the air forwards. Often an AC can direct its flow. If so, direct it so that no cold air actually blows onto you.
- Use a canopy bed with a light fabric above. This will disperse the flowing cold air and stop it from blowing directly onto you.
- Visually conceal the AC, ideally by hiding it behind louvres, but at the very least by painting your walls a colour that allows the machine to blend in. This does not solve the cold air issue, but mentally lightens it.
- Add warming elements to your room, like cosy lamps and warm colours and textiles to balance out the cold.
- This applies to other types of machinery; for example, if your room is in a basement, always try to conceal the ducting and pipes.

19

# There's space under my stairs, I'll place my desk there

**Rating:**

Feng shui says... working under the stairs will stunt your growth and slice your luck to bits.

### Why

Stairs are structurally substantial, and being under them can feel heavy and overwhelming. The angled ceiling creates an awkward space, often forcing you to hunch or sit lower than normal. If the stairs have open treads, each step may appear like a blade hanging overhead, creating a constant sense of pressure or aggression. Most importantly, stairs represent constant movement. Sitting beneath them symbolises people walking over you and stepping on your head, which is a classic feng shui metaphor for being suppressed and disrespected in life and work. Over time, this can affect confidence, focus and progress, which is why the space under the stairs is considered one of the worst places for anything.

### Fix it!

Don't use the space under a staircase for any activity – you don't want to spend time there.

- Avoid placing your desk, couch or reading nook under the stairs, and never allow anyone to sleep there.
- Use it for storage. The space under the stairs is not only great for storage, but solves another feng shui issue – the aggressive yet flimsy appearance of exposed stair treads. Closing up the space can make the staircase feel calmer and more stable.
- Alternatives to closed storage include a cabinet to display your items, or even a drinks bar.
- It could occasionally work as a pet corner if your pets don't mind the limited space or light. Usually, pets prefer to hang out with people, so this works only if it is adjacent to living areas.
- If you absolutely have to use the underside of your stairs for a study area, ensure it is finished nicely, and design your desk to fit into the alcove. Most importantly, add lights to illuminate the space so it does not feel dark or heavy, position yourself away from the lowest point of the stairs, and keep your head clear of overhangs.

20

# The corner of a wall is pointing right at me, I keep looking at it

**Rating:** 

Feng shui says... protruding corners and edges of walls pointing at you mean hidden hostility towards you.

**Why**

Feng shui dislikes anything that pokes at you, like sharp corners or hard edges. These are known as poison arrows which carry sha chi or 'killing energy'. The most obvious examples are exposed pointy knives or open shelves, but architectural features can do the same thing. This includes protruding corners of 'L' shaped rooms, stray columns, or the open edge of a large built-in wardrobe. This can also be felt outside the home, where a neighbouring building might have its pointy edge facing your window. While these are common in modern architecture, it can feel subtly unsettling when they point at you. Over time, this low-level tension can cause enough irritation to affect your overall calm in the space.

**Fix it!**

Shield yourself from any kind of pointy corner and reduce visual impact.

- Avoid awkward layouts. When designing or choosing a home, avoid complicated floor plans with many corridors or 'L'-shaped rooms. If there are columns, hide them in walls rather than leaving them exposed.
- Fill gaps with storage. Odd recesses and indents are great places for built-in storage: not only does it level out the annoying corners, but also makes these spaces functional.
- Round off the corners by making them curved. This is not easy, but if you are renovating, it can make your home look architecturally interesting as well.
- Reposition yourself. Avoid sitting or sleeping directly in line with a corner. For example, if you turn the corner into a seating nook, this transforms the aggression: you're inside the corner, rather than being targeted by it.
- Visually block corners with plants or lamps, or paint your walls in a way that they blend in or disappear.
- For pointy corners outside the house, placing plants or sheer curtains in your windows will diffuse the energy.

21

# My office is in a windowless nook, I can't wait to finish work

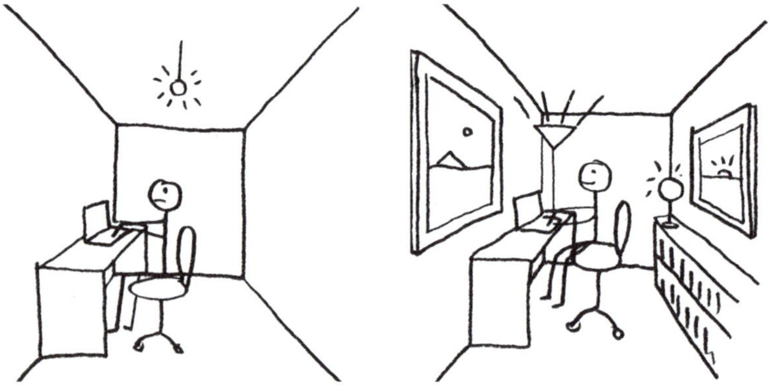

**Rating:**

Feng shui says... being in a room with no windows will block all your opportunities and make you feel isolated.

**Why**

Humans are naturally drawn to light, air and open views. A room without windows is like a tomb: it removes all connection with the world outside and, symbolically, any opportunities. This causes you to feel disorientated and even hopeless, losing track of both time and motivation. Having no windows will also create a sense of claustrophobia and anxiety. The health effects of having no natural light are increased melatonin and decreased serotonin, reducing your energy and making you feel tired. This applies to basements or rooms in the middle of the house with no access to natural light as well.

**Fix it!**

There are two ways to address a windowless room: you can either use it for something that does not need light, or add as much energy as possible.

- Limit your use of the room to non-critical functions. Make it a movie room, gym, spa or space for specific hobbies like photography or recording music – but not sleeping. Note that these are also time-limited functions, where you leave after you finish the movie or workout.
- Use layered lighting. If you have to use a windowless room for an important space, like a living room, use lots of indirect lights. If you have lamps facing up, you'll create a soft glow, which makes a room feel warm and cosy. A single pendant hanging high above will emphasise the four enclosing walls – so don't do that!
- If you need to work in the room, use reflected ambient light. This creates an even, soft glow which will reduce the feeling of confinement. Do this by shining a strong light onto your ceiling or walls so the light bounces back.
- Add other sources of energy, like aquariums or plants with grow-lights. These mimic the vitality of the outside world.
- Use mirrors or hang artwork. Strategically positioned, mirrors can open your space further and add movement and energy. Hang artwork that shows landscapes, as this can behave like a window to the outside world.

# I live in a modern apartment with huge windows everywhere

**Rating:**

Feng shui says... too many giant windows will cause all your fortune to leak away.

### Why

In feng shui, your home is a place where energy enters your life. When there are too many windows, all this energy will leak out. The idea of fortune 'leaking away' through windows comes from the assumption that your assets are on show for anyone to see, which can invite envy or judgment from others. Practically, if there are too many openings, you may feel exposed and vulnerable. This lack of privacy keeps you on alert, making it difficult to fully relax. Even if the view is beautiful and quiet, it can still distract your mind and draw your attention, preventing focus.

### Fix it!

Try to create privacy and control what people outside can see, while still maintaining the view that brings you joy.

- Add curtains or blinds to control the amount of light and exposure while softening the energy.
- Use bottom-up blinds or cafe curtains if you are on the ground floor with people walking by. This way they can no longer see inside while you can still see the sky.
- Shielding the lower half of the windows is a good idea, even if you're not on the ground floor. Use low consoles or cabinets to buffer the lower half of the windows to create a sense of distance.
- Prioritise the view. If there are windows on more than one side, choose the window with the better view to focus on, and cover the others.
- Frame your windows with tall plants to slow the energy and tighten the view.
- Position yourself further away from the windows. For example, move your couch or your bed deeper inside the room to feel less exposed.
- Use warm, heavier textures and materials to create cosy vibes and anchor the energy inside the room.

23

# I have big double-height ceilings and it does not feel cosy

**Rating:** 

Feng shui says... rooms with high ceilings may lead to leakages of wealth.

**Why**

The home is meant to offer grounding support and allow you to connect intimately with yourself and your family. When spaces are too big and grand, they can make us feel small or insignificant, leading to overstimulation and restlessness. In feng shui terms, this is described as energy being dispersed rather than held. Trying to focus, unwind or relax is more challenging in these spaces. We end up occupying the space in a transient way, much like waiting in a hotel lobby, which is grand and impressive, but not somewhere you can naturally settle. And, like in a hotel lobby, once your friend comes, you can't wait to move on to a 'proper' space to sit.

**Fix it!**

Make your double-height space supported and intimate.

- Choose the right function for the space. Tall rooms are great for formal living or reception rooms. Watching TV or relaxing should be in a more intimate space if you have the option.
- Use a less formal layout. Instead of two facing couches, try to have a cosy modular sofa that allows lounging and casual sitting, and anchor it with a big fluffy rug. Have a big coffee table or multiple small tables so you don't feel too far from them.
- Make the space feel more intimate. Add tall plants or arching lamps close to seating areas.
- Don't forget about the space above you. Hang a chandelier to lower the perceived ceiling height, though always have a table under the chandelier to anchor it (and make sure no one is sitting under it).
- Fill the walls. Punctuate the huge walls with decorative items like curtains that soften, mouldings that add interest, or large artwork to break the monotony and scale of the space.
- Resist overhead storage. Using the upper walls for storage increases visual pressure and makes the room more overwhelming. Tall bookcases or shelving can work if they fill out the entire wall.

24

# I plan to install skylights all over my home for more light

**Rating:** 

Feng shui says... skylights in the wrong rooms can cause you to feel exposed and your emotions to become unstable.

**Why**

Skylights are great for bringing in natural light, especially in darker homes. However, they need to be thoughtfully placed. The roof of your home symbolises protection. Skylights can therefore be seen as making holes in your protective shield. Practically speaking, when you are in a room with a large skylight, you might feel overly exposed to the elements, or even to your neighbours, if they are higher than you. Instead of feeling held and cosy, you might feel pulled up into the sky. At night, this unease can grow even stronger as skylights can appear like a dark void above you.

**Fix it!**

Skylights are best located where openness is desired but not where you want calm and grounding.

- The best locations for skylights are transitional or functional spaces such as bathrooms, hallways, staircases, kitchens, breakfast areas or casual family spaces. Recreation rooms or basements can benefit from them too.
- Avoid skylights in restful or focused rooms. Bedrooms, study rooms, formal living rooms or dining rooms are where you want to feel grounded and contained. In study rooms, skylights can be distracting and you might lose focus.
- Entrances can look nice with skylights, but this might allow energy to rush out, making your home feel airy and hollow. In entrances, choose circular skylights to create a sense of containment.
- Anchor the space. If you do have a huge skylight over your main living space, bring the eye down with large, solid elements like a hefty dining or coffee table and a nice chandelier to 'hold' the energy within the room.
- If you are designing your house and have to add a skylight in a bedroom or living room, use it thoughtfully, for example locating it more towards the side rather than right in the middle, and ensuring key furniture is not directly under it.

25

# My front door is made of glass, I hope nobody breaks in

**Rating:**

Feng shui says... a glass front door would lead to misfortune entering your life.

### Why

Your main entrance is the primary entry point to your home, where chi or energy enters your home and your life. In feng shui, your front door should be strong and solid, not only to protect you from unwanted energy, but also to create a clear and confident sense of arrival. When the door is transparent, this important threshold disappears. Practically anyone from the street can see right into your home, making you feel exposed and vulnerable: you can no longer walk around your own home naked! Even in a safe neighbourhood, a glass door means you won't have a sense of privacy and personal space, and you may feel constantly observed rather than protected.

### Fix it!

Change your door to a strong, solid one, or make it as protected as possible.

- Hang curtains or blinds, or apply frosted film so outsiders cannot see in.
- Add door guardians, such as a pair of stone lions, elephants or even plants to flank the outside of your front door. These make the home feel guarded and occupied, which discourages people from looking in.
- Add a light to your porch; when it switches on at night, it will be more difficult to see in.
- If you want a glass door, limit the glass. Have windows flanking the door instead, or choose a design where only the top half is glass and the bottom is still solid.
- Avoid clear glass. Regardless of design, ensure the glass is frosted or stained so it is impossible to see through. Use thick safety glass to make your door feel more secure.

# There are a million doors in my room, even I get confused

**Rating:**

Feng shui says... a room with many doors will cause anxiety and scattered feelings.

**Why**

A door is a big source of energy, as we associate it with people coming and going (because of this, you should position yourself as far from doors as possible, as a general rule!). Now, imagine your room is punctured with two, three, four, five doors. Not only does this make furniture placement difficult, it also reduces the sense of enclosure and safety that a room is meant to provide. You are instead distracted by all these doors, and subconsciously more alert than necessary. Even if we know that some doors lead to closets or bathrooms, their presence can be visually and energetically disruptive.

**Fix it!**

Manage the energy of multiple doors and your own position in relation to them.

- Draw out and analyse the circulation paths leading out from each door, and place key pieces of furniture – like your bed – so that none of that movement energy points towards you.
- For closet or bathroom doors, paint them the same colour as the walls so they blend into the room.
- Keep bathroom doors closed at all times, or hang door curtains to further block out the toilet energy. If your bathroom is a Jack and Jill bathroom (shared access from two bedrooms), add a lock so you can control access to your room.
- Hang heavy, full-length curtains on balcony, garden or terrace doors to create a sense of enclosure when you need it, especially at night.
- Your main door should be the only door that is prominent.

# FURNITURE ARRANGEMENT

# AND

# PLACEMENT

27

# My feet point at the door, I can’t sleep

**Rating:**

Feng shui says... sleeping with your feet to the door means that you will die (sooner).

### Why

A door is highly energetic and the bed should never be too close to it, but pointing your feet at it amplifies that feeling. This is a vulnerable position: if anyone enters the room, you will be caught unprepared, perhaps in embarrassing situations! Apart from this practical reason, there are many superstitious connections. For example, in Chinese funerals, the coffin is placed with the feet pointing to the door to symbolise a person's exit from life. Or consider that when a baby is born, the feet exiting first is dangerous. These practical and emotional connections mean that sleeping this way could affect your ability to rest.

### Fix it!

Of course, try to avoid such a layout, but if that's not possible, reduce exposure and protect yourself as much as possible.

- Avoid being directly in line with the door. Try to push the bed left or right slightly so you are off the door's path.
- Cover the door as much as you can by hanging a curtain or painting the door the same colour as the wall so it blends in.
- Choose a bed that offers privacy and protection: one that has a high footboard, so you feel like there is something between you and the door.
- Create a room within a room by having a four-poster bed with curtains, so you feel protected.
- Create a physical block: place a screen or bench between the bed and the door.
- Hang a crystal between the door and bed as a last resort. This is said to absorb and soften the incoming energy.

28

# My bed head is against the window and the wind blows on my face

**Rating:**

Feng shui says... if you sleep with a window behind you, you will have restless nights with wild dreams and nightmares.

### Why

Sleep is a time when you should feel fully supported and protected. A solid wall behind you symbolises stability and safety. Having a window there instead has the opposite effect: you'll not only feel a lack of support, but be more vulnerable because the only thing between you and the wild animals outside is a thin pane of glass. Light and noise might permeate through the windows, adding another layer of energy. All this will subconsciously put you on guard, leading to lighter sleep and preventing you from fully relaxing. The effect of the window is, however, dependent on the view it has. For example, a window facing a blank wall might feel more stable than a window that opens onto the street with people walking by. That said, having the bed against a wall is still best. Note that side windows are acceptable, even if they are on the same wall as the bed, as long as they are not directly behind you.

### Fix it!

The goal is to make the window feel as solid and stable as possible by removing its energetic impact.

- Hang heavy blackout curtains to totally block or cover the window. Try not to allow any light to pass.
- Choose a high and solid headboard; this mimics a wall and protects you from behind.
- Permanently shut the window with drywall or even a screen. This is a big move, but if you never use it, or if the window is high up with no view, there is nothing to lose. Note this should only be done if there is an alternative window in the room.
- Use bottom-up blinds or cafe curtains if you want to showcase the view behind you but still have some privacy. Blocking the bottom half is usually enough to make you feel adequately protected.

29

# I sleep with my feet facing out the window and it wakes me up

**Rating:**

Feng shui says... sleeping with your feet towards a window will cause your energy to be sucked out.

**Why**

While you will not actually become weaker from sleeping with your feet to the window, it might affect how soundly you rest. The reason is that a big window is a source of energy: it allows light, sound and connection to the outside world. At the same time, the feet are associated with stability, being connected to the ground. So having a big bright window right where your feet are would make you feel vulnerable and exposed, even giving you the sense of sleeping upside down or being 'pulled' out of the window.

**Fix it!**

Regulate and reduce the amount of energy coming through the window when you sleep.

- Reposition your bed so that the window is to your side. However, windows in front are still better than having the windows behind you.
- Block the window with thick curtains or even blinds, especially when you are sleeping. This gives an energetic shield, and reinforces your sense of protection.
- If you're designing your bedroom, choose the right window size. Short, wider windows offer more protection than narrow, tall windows.
- Use a bed with a footboard: this will act like a barrier between you and the window, holding your energy in place while you sleep.
- Place a piece of furniture like a bench in front of the bed or a low dresser under the window. This will give a sense of distance and protection.
- Add table lamps beside your bed. This sounds unrelated, but the light will balance out the energy from the windows.
- Centre your bed to the window; this is better than having half of it facing a wall and the other half facing out the window.

# My bed is pushed all the way into the corner, it's cosy but a bit lonely

**Rating:**

Feng shui says... if two people are sharing this bed, one of you will feel cornered; if you're single, you will stay single forever.

**Why**

In feng shui, the bed should be centred, with side tables and lamps on both sides, representing balance and companionship. When a shared bed is pushed to one corner, getting in means climbing over your partner, which might make you feel trapped or less important than them. In the long run, this may develop into unnecessary tension. If you are single, a bed in the corner would suggest that the bed is only meant for one, and you subconsciously give yourself the signal that you are not ready for a partner. That said, if you actually want to stay single, then having your bed in a corner is good. This applies especially to young kids. Their focus is on self-development, so in a kid's room it is actually good to place a single bed in the corner to symbolise independence over partnership.

**Fix it!**

This is only worth 'fixing' if you are in a relationship or if you want to be partnered with someone.

- Position the bed so there is space on both sides. Even a little gap of 30cm or a foot is enough for someone to pass through. Have a side table and a lamp on each side so both people have their space.
- If you can't fit a side table, make sure the inner side is still usable by adding a thin floor lamp and maybe a small shelf. This visually gives the impression of balance while making both sides functional.
- Get a larger bed. If the bed needs to be in the corner, a generous size gives more space for both people, reducing that cornered feeling.
- Create an alternative space for companionship. If your bed is in the corner, you can still place a loveseat or a pair of armchairs in your room to invite a partner to hang out with you.
- Use decor to encourage love. Even if the bed does not scream romance, you can add accessories or artwork in pairs, like a pair of lovebirds, or even using sweet, pinkish tones in your textiles. These other cues are just as effective in reminding you that your room is ready for love.

31

# The toilet is by my bed, I wake up every time my partner flushes

**Rating:** 

Feng shui says... if you sleep against a bathroom wall, you will gradually suffer from illnesses.

**Why**

A bathroom is where we wash and go to the toilet. With its water and waste pipes, it is considered a damp and dirty place, whereas our sleeping areas should be dry and protected. Having them close to each other or, worse still, with your bed back-to-back to the toilet, is bad. Traditional feng shui texts might even suggest avoiding ensuites entirely, to ensure there is no water close to the bed. Since modern plumbing and ventilation systems have improved hygiene significantly, the issue today is more psychological and sensory. Hearing your partner poop or feeling the vibration of the toilet flushing in the middle of the night can be disruptive enough to affect your rest.

**Fix it!**

Add distance and protection between your bed and the toilet.

- Design the bathroom to minimise disruption. If you are renovating, place the toilet away from shared bedroom walls and minimise the run of toilet pipes along those walls. Even better, separate the toilet into its own cubicle within the bathroom.

- Avoid placing the bed directly against the bathroom wall and instead position wardrobes or storage units along the shared wall to act as a buffer. If the bed must go there, the most important thing is to avoid it lining up with the toilet.

- Use a thick, solid headboard. A padded headboard also helps absorb sound and vibration, creating a stronger sense of protection.

- Keep the bathroom dry and well ventilated. Check that there are no leaks, use warm lighting, and ensure good airflow. Adding plants can help absorb excess moisture.

- Keep the bathroom door closed at all times and put the toilet seat down when not in use.

- Avoid water imagery in the bedroom, especially behind the bed. Choose earthy artwork to symbolically 'absorb' excess water energy.

32

# Can I sleep on the floor? They do it in Asia and it looks cute

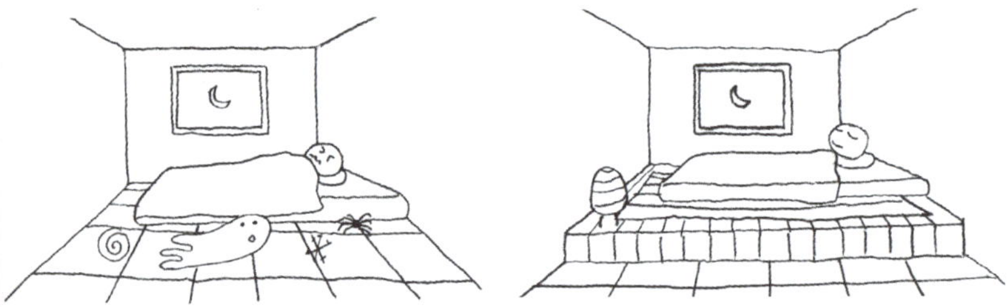

**Rating:** 

Feng shui says... sleeping on the floor can affect your sense of authority in life and your physical wellbeing.

## Why

In Chinese folk belief, ghosts are said to move close to the ground, which is why traditional temples often have raised thresholds. But this is really a metaphor for how the earth, with its damp soil and association with burials, can carry excessive yin energy when we have prolonged contact with it. Explained practically, floors can be draughtier and colder, and this does actually draw out your body's warmth over time, particularly if your floors are made of tiles or if you are on the ground floor. You might be wondering, but what about people in Japan who sleep on the floor? Traditionally, Japanese people sleep on tatami, which are insulating, breathable mats that are – most importantly – placed on floors that are slightly raised above the main circulation paths of the house. So, while they are close to the ground, they are never directly exposed to it.

## Fix it!

If you like to sleep low, here are a few rules to keep you safe and comfortable.

- Avoid sleeping directly on the floor. Use a raised platform, futon base or low bed frame to create some separation from the ground.
- Stay away from the doors and walking paths, as these are high-energy routes. Choose the deepest, safest corners of the room.
- Use thick rugs, especially if your floor is concrete or tiled. Rugs can insulate and protect you from the chills of the floor, as well as help mark out the different zones.
- Sleep on an upper level of the home. It is more acceptable to be on the floor if you are already on an elevated level of the house.
- Avoid tall furniture or objects towering over you. This will amplify the feeling of being undesirably low. Add low-level lighting to create cosiness.

# The door is behind me when I work, it's so distracting

**Rating:** 

Feng shui says... working with a door behind you means that your co-workers will backstab and gossip about you.

**Why**

The door is a major source of energy since it's where people come in and out of the room. So when you sit with your back towards it, you will feel exposed. Anyone could come in at any moment, giving you very little time to react. Even if there is nobody else in the house, the very presence of this portal right behind you will still cause you to be on alert – especially if the door is open or even slightly ajar. In a workspace, where your co-workers are walking around behind you, you might feel like things are happening without your knowledge: conversations or decisions happening behind your back, subtly making you feel like you lack control.

**Fix it!**

The main problem is that you feel watched from behind, so the trick is to restore awareness and control.

- Avoid having your back square on to the door. For example, if you can have an 'L'-shaped desk, you might be able to turn your body at an angle, so the door is more towards your side than behind.
- Place a mirror on your desk. This sounds strange, but it acts like a rearview mirror, so you can see anyone who is sneaking up behind you.
- Place a barrier like a piece of furniture between you and the door. If the room is big enough, you might place a little table or seating area behind you; this not only invites collaboration but also forms a barrier that distances you from the door.
- Add an audible cue to let you know someone is close or coming in, such as a bell or bead curtains over the door.

# There's nowhere else for my desk to go but facing the wall

**Rating:** 

Feng shui says... when you work facing a wall, you lose sight of what's ahead, missing opportunities and grinding through life.

### Why

In feng shui it is important to always have openness in front of you. This is symbolised by the five animals: your front is the bird, representing openness and flight. When you work facing a wall, you feel blocked and oblivious to what is happening. It's a bit like driving down a road with a large truck right in front of you; it's so big that you can't see what's ahead. Practically, when you face a wall, you limit your imagination. All you can think of is your work, making it feel monotonous and meaningless, and you won't ever feel inspired or creative.

### Fix it!

Reduce the feeling of staring at a wall to allow you to feel inspired.

- Facing a screen helps. Remember, feng shui is old, and people in the past didn't have computer screens. In modern times, when we have a big screen to look at, it does behave like a window to the world, so it's not so bad.

- Float your desk. Reposition it so the wall is behind you, and you are facing towards the main space in front of you. If you are worried about seeing the cables, sort it! Use cable management and consolidate them to one side.

- Sit close to a window. Having a window close by allows you to turn and look out at the view, giving a sense of openness.

- Choose a deeper desk. More depth means you won't feel so pressed against the wall. A wider desk can help you spread sideways.

- Hang art. A nice picture on the wall in front of you can behave like a window and carry your imagination. Avoid shelves above, which may further press down on the wall.

# What background should I use for virtual meetings?

**Rating:** 

Feng shui says... your choice of background can affect your reputation and authority.

### Why

While virtual meetings never existed in ancient China, your backdrop, real or virtual, can influence how you are seen in the eyes of others. If you use your default company background with their logo, you might appear soulless and overly associated with your employer. If you use a blurred background, it suggests that you are hiding something, or you're not fully ready to engage. If you show your messy kitchen with your kids running around, it signals chaos and that work is not your top priority. If you have all your certificates and achievements hanging behind you, you might appear boastful or intimidating. The best background is curated: perhaps a piece of art next to some shelves decorated with carefully selected objects and books. This shows your taste and knowledge without revealing too much or being distracting during the meeting.

### Fix it!

Create a background which represents you and how you want others to perceive you.

- Position yourself so there is a wall behind you, not the open room.
- Don't leave the wall blank – you will look like you are a hostage! Decorate your background with art or books. Be mindful of your choice of art: what you hang behind you says a lot.
- Keep shelves below shoulder height. This way the storage will not overwhelm you. If you do have a full-height bookcase behind you, place lighter decorative objects on the upper levels.
- Use good lighting to illuminate your face and avoid having a window behind you to prevent backlighting.
- If you can't do the above, remember that a blurred background is still better than a messy room, or an overly standard virtual background like a fake living room or the Golden Gate Bridge!

36

# The door is right next to me as I work

**Rating:** 

Feng shui says... sleeping or working with a door right next to you will cause disturbance and lack of control.

**Why**

Ever notice how the more important the person, the deeper in their study/office they are positioned? That's because it is safer and they are less likely to be bothered by interruptions. If you sit right by the door, it can make you feel like a receptionist. If you sleep by the door, you will feel like you're not able to fully settle into your own room. In feng shui, a door represents movement and change, and we're easily distracted by anything happening there. Even if nobody is using the door, it still causes us to feel subconsciously alert, preventing us from fully focusing on our task. Over time, this heightened alertness can leave us drained and fatigued. Not all doors are equal, though: entry doors are the most disruptive, while closet doors are far less of an issue. That said, it's still best to hide them to reduce the energy.

**Fix it!**

Shift your bed or desk away from the door, or create a sense of perceived distance.

- Change the door swing so it opens away from you. This will help you feel more protected, even if the door is open. Take note of where the light switches are before doing this.
- Add lamps or plants between you and the door to soften the movement energy.
- For beds, choose headboards with a wing design to protect the sides; for seating, choose armchairs instead of stools to embrace you more.
- Use a screen to block the path between you and the door. A low bookshelf can work too.
- Paint the door the same colour as the walls to make it less apparent, or hang a curtain to maintain privacy even when the door is open.
- Note that it is still better to sit or sleep near the door than to work with your back to it or sleep with your feet pointing towards it.

# My sofa is floating in the middle of the room

**Rating:** 

Feng shui says... a sofa floating in the middle of the room will cause the family to lack grounding.

**Why**

After a long day you probably want to chill out on your sofa and unwind, as it is where you can recover, recharge and connect with family. But when your sofa is in the middle of the living space with nothing behind, it can make you feel exposed, vulnerable and unable to fully relax. If you can't feel comfortable there, it often means there is nowhere else to relax at home, which can affect opportunities for family connections. In contrast, a sofa against a wall gives a sense of containment, safety and cosiness, where everyone can truly settle in and spend time together. It does depend on what is behind you, though. For example, if your sofa is floating to allow space to access a bookshelf, it is much less energetic than having the front door or main walking pathways behind you, and isn't as bad.

**Fix it!**

Reduce the amount of energy coming from behind the sofa as much as possible.

- The best option is to reposition the sofa. Try placing it against a wall. Often the reason people float sofas is because of the TV, but it may be worth reconsidering the TV placement in the name of comfort.
- Reduce the energy behind the sofa. Not all floating sofas are equal! Position it so that there is as little movement behind you as possible. For example, having a dining table behind the sofa is better than having the main walking path through the room behind you.
- Create support for the sofa by placing a low console, bench or shelf behind it. This provides backing and creates space between you and the people walking behind.
- Hang a decorative mirror in front of the sofa. That means that when you're lounging, you'll still be able to see what's happening behind like it's a rearview mirror, giving you a greater sense of control in the room.

# The window is behind my sofa, everyone can see what I'm watching

**Rating:** 😣😣😣

Feng shui says... a large window directly behind you means unreliable support from others.

**Why**

When you are sleeping, a window behind you gives off energy, making you feel vulnerable. When you are focusing, whether that's on work or a TV show, a window behind you becomes a distraction, both physically and mentally. The physical problems include light reflecting off your screen, making it hard to see; any movement behind will distract you; and, if you are having virtual meetings, the backlight will put you in shadow. Mentally, having a window behind you as you try to focus will make you feel watched, especially if you have neighbours facing you or you live on the ground floor. This is even more apparent at night, when your living room is all lit up like a fish tank, and your TV or screen becomes a beacon, broadcasting your viewing choices to the street. In a way, revealing your preferences or work can feel more exposing than showing your face, turning what's meant to be relaxation or focus time into an emotional rollercoaster.

**Fix it!**

The goal is to regain a sense of support and privacy and reduce distractions.

- Reposition your seating so that your back is not directly to the window, especially for workstations.
- Block or soften the window with curtains or blinds. If you are on the ground floor, use bottom-up blinds or cafe curtains to provide permanent privacy without blocking the sky.
- Use a high-backed sofa or furniture to create more support. If possible, add a low console behind.
- Add visual weight in front of you, such as a large coffee table with decorations on it, to help you forget about the energy behind.
- Decorate your windowsill with plants and objects to create a buffer between you and the window.
- Close the curtains at night, preventing anyone outside from looking in and seeing what you are watching, giving you privacy and peace of mind.

# My dining table is against the wall, it's so hard to get around

**Rating:** 

Feng shui says... a dining table pushed to the wall can cause disharmony and limited abundance.

**Why**

A dining table represents the heart of the home and is where the family gathers. It is therefore important that the table feels central and anchored, and allows everyone equal access to the food and each other. When the table is squeezed against a wall, whether you've pushed the short end or the long end of the table against it, this opens up the possibility that someone will have to sit at the end, slightly removed from the main group. This makes that person feel excluded or overlooked. Practically speaking, when the table is pushed to a wall, it becomes harder for people to sit down comfortably or, especially in Asian cuisine, reach for shared food. These may seem like small inconveniences, but over time they can discourage use. Ultimately, a table is more than just a place to eat: it represents the family and should allow comfortable gathering and connection.

**Fix it!**

Avoid pushing your table against a wall, but if space is limited, reduce the sense of imbalance.

- Do not place things where the table touches the wall, as that will make it feel like a dumping ground for clutter. Keep the table clear and usable.
- If you've pushed the long edge against a wall, hang a mirror to open the closed side. Or, if the short edge is against the wall, hang a piece of art to balance the end.
- Ensure the person sitting at the end has slightly more space, so they don't feel squeezed.
- Pushing the short edge of the table against the wall is better than the long edge, and pushing it against a kitchen island is better than pushing it against a wall.
- Hang a pendant light over the table to suggest a central focus that anchors the whole table equally.
- Consider round tables: they take up less room and allow for the table to float in the middle of smaller spaces.

40

# I live alone in a big house, so there are many empty rooms

**Rating:** 

Feng shui says... an empty room breeds stagnant energy, which invites unwanted guests.

**Why**

An empty room that is not used collects dust and stale air. This feeling of stillness is overly yin, or lacking human warmth. In feng shui, all rooms in the home should be active and used. I don't mean rooms with a purpose that you don't use that much: a home gym might only be used once a week, but its presence encourages vitality. Another type of room to avoid is one that is 'waiting'. Guest rooms with their beds made up suggest that the room belongs to someone: fine if you have regular guests, but if there is no clear occupant, Chinese folk belief says that such spaces may invite ghosts. Similarly, rooms left empty for children who do not yet exist should be avoided, because this may create emotional pressure rather than being an invitation.

**Fix it!**

Never leave a room empty or waiting.

- Use the room for something. Think light, flexible purposes like a stretching room. All you need is a floormat, some medicine balls or rollers, and a few plants. The room does not need to be packed; intention alone is enough to activate the space and breathe life into it.
- Think of ways to use the room that will enrich your life, like a gym, TV room or hobby room. You might not need these spaces, or even use them regularly, but their presence reflects self-care and personal growth.
- Use it for storage (thoughtfully!). While you should never call it a storeroom, you can still use this now activated space to store and display items, like books or collectibles. Remember, the point is to create a room you will use.
- Enter the room daily. Open the windows to freshen it, and perhaps add a plant so you go in to water and check on it every day.
- If you do want to keep it as a guest room, but you only have the occasional visitor, push the bed to a corner and dress it up so it looks more like a daybed or reading nook. That will show that the room clearly belongs to you first, and you are 'allowed' to enter and use it.

# COMPASS

# AND

# SUPERSTITION

41

# I'm apparently an East person but my home faces West, which is unlucky

**Rating:**

Feng shui says... if your home faces your unlucky direction, it could mean anything from daily obstacles to a lifetime of bad luck.

**Why**

In feng shui, each compass direction has its own energy. Some traditions suggest that directions affect you differently, depending on when you are born. It's like being born on a sunny day: that means you will love sunshine and hate the rain, and choosing a house that faces the 'wrong' direction is like choosing a house where it's always raining. Superstitions aside, the practical truth is how it makes you feel. If you love sunshine, and you bought a north-facing home (or south, depending on your location), being constantly in shadow might make you feel sad. Conversely, if you dislike glaring afternoon sun and your home faces west, you might feel the need to close the curtains to protect yourself. The direction of your home is determined by your front door if it's a house, or the largest window in your living space if it's an apartment.

**Fix it!**

If your home faces a direction that drains you energetically, make adjustments to soften its impact.

- Spend more time facing your favourite direction. If your home has rooms facing different sides, try to spend most time in the room that you enjoy more. For example, if you love sun, but your study room faces north, while your bedroom faces south (and you're in the Northern Hemisphere), swap their functions.
- Use window treatments to adjust the energy. If the room is too bright and sunny, use blinds and curtains to give shade, or sit deeper inside the room. If the light is too dim, place yourself right by the window.
- Position yourself towards directions that energise you. If you follow compass feng shui, you can orient your bed or desk towards your personal 'lucky' direction, even if the room faces a less ideal side.
- Prioritise flow and comfort. While compass feng shui considers personal lucky directions, it is widely accepted that form feng shui, which focuses on how the immediate energy of your home flows, is more important. Trust your instincts and create a space that feels right for you.

# What is a money corner and what if I mess it up?

**Rating:** 

Feng shui says... the money corner, if done well, will attract wealth and prosperity to your home.

**Why**

In every home, there is a corner that has the greatest visual and psychological effect on you: this is the money corner, the most auspicious part of your home. Your money corner is the deepest corner of your home visible from the entrance. It should be in the main living space and close to natural light. If your living room is not visible from the entrance, you may have two money corners, one in a visible spot, and another in the main living area. The reason is that wealth needs to 'see' its way into your home, and once it arrives, should remain present and visible. This is not purely magic. Looking at a beautifully arranged money corner gives a nudge or affirmation that your home is in a good place, and you the confidence to strive for more prosperity outside the home. Conversely, if this corner is full of haphazard clutter, it subtly reminds you that your life is in disarray and dampens your motivation.

**Fix it!**

Find your money corner, and ensure that it looks beautiful and welcoming.

- Make it attractive. Wealth is usually pretty, shiny, golden and sparkling, and your corner needs to showcase beautiful objects and look well thought-out (no unfinished paint jobs here). Bonus points if you include an object that moves and draws your attention, like the Japanese lucky cat.
- It should represent growth. A bowl of coins or a piggy bank which you actively use by adding spare change will represent continual growth. A healthy plant that is alive and thriving reinforces this idea.
- It should symbolise wealth. Choose items that culturally represent prosperity. In feng shui, examples include the money frog, a creature that loved to hoard golden coins, or the pixiu, mythical beasts that love eating gold and jewels, but are unable to poop them out because they have no anus. These are examples – only use something that resonates with you.
- Don't neglect it! Avoid making it your junk corner or putting things that are off-putting there, like your cat's litter box. If the corner is near a bathroom, close the bathroom door; if it's in front of the kitchen, keep the space tidy and decorated with symbols of abundance, like a bowl of fruit.

# I sleep with my head to the North, is that bad luck?

**Rating:** 

Feng shui says... sleeping with your head to the North is associated with death in some cultures.

**Why**

In Vastu Shastra, the Indian sister of feng shui, sleeping with your head to the north is considered inauspicious because it means your body is pointing towards the south, the direction associated with death. In Hindu tradition, the dead are laid facing south as Yama, the god of death, is believed to rule this direction. Avoiding sleeping with your head to the north is also observed in Japanese Buddhist custom, as the dead are traditionally placed with their heads pointing north. Some people make the argument that sleeping with your head to the north goes against the Earth's magnetic field, but there is no real scientific evidence to support this. Interestingly, feng shui does not mention this, nor does it associate the south with death. In fact, feng shui links the south with prosperity, which seems to contradict the ideas of Vastu. One reason is geography. China is further north, so the sun's warmth is much desired, while India is located closer to the equator, where the sun's more persistent energy becomes draining, hence the less favourable associations. This is to say: when heeding advice, it helps to understand the cultural context before panicking.

**Fix it!**

Ultimately, you should sleep in a way that supports your mind and body, so choose a position to give you the calm you need.

- Regardless of compass direction, prioritise how the room feels. Observe where the doors and windows are, and sleep in the command position of the room, away from any energy flow. This is more important than whether you're north or south, because this you can actually feel.
- Prioritise peace of mind too. The most important thing of all is comfort, both physical and mental. If you feel uneasy knowing your head is facing north, trust your instincts and change the position of your bed. But remember that a calm mind is more important than following any rule perfectly.

44

# My house number is 4 and my mum says it means death

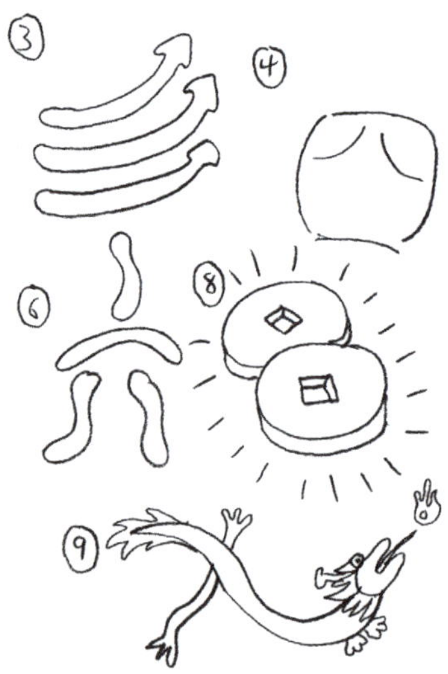


**Rating:**

Feng shui says... if your address is the number 4, bad luck and misfortune will befall you.

**Why**

The Chinese language is largely homophonic, where different characters can share the same sound. This means that numbers, when read aloud, are often associated with words that sound similar. Here are some of the stronger number associations:

3 – 三 (sān) – life – symbolically associated with 生 (shēng)
4 – 四 (sì) – death – homophone of 死 (sǐ)
6 – 六 (liù) – smooth – homophone of 流 (liú)
8 – 八 (baat) – prosperity – homophone of 发 (faat) in Cantonese
9 – 九 (jiǔ) – longevity – homophone of 久 (jiǔ)

Because of this, the Chinese place a strong importance on numerology, and identical houses can command different prices simply based on their door numbers. As a result, homes with the number 4 are often avoided because of its association with death and bad luck. Of course, the number is just a number, and does not literally cause death or misfortune. The real issue is your emotional attachment to it. Once you believe that the number is bad for you, your mind becomes anxious and biased towards negative events, and sure enough, bad things will start to feel more frequent. Conversely, if I told you that your home has an auspicious door number, you might feel a surge of confidence, and positivity would follow.

**Fix it!**

If your house has a bad number, try shifting its meaning through reframing.

- Choose a beautifully crafted door plate to highlight the appearance of your door, rather than the number.
- Give your home a name, for example, Honey Cottage. While the number may be used for postage, you do not need to emotionally engage with it.
- Reframe your mind. For example, 4 may mean death, but it can also mean structure and stability. Choose a meaning that supports you and believe in it.

# I want an altar to pray, is it allowed in my bedroom?

**Rating:** 

Feng shui says... altars or shrines in the bedroom will restrict intimacy and make you feel watched.

**Why**

A bedroom is a calm and private space where we not only rest, but where our most intimate feelings and actions take place. An altar or shrine, on the other hand, carries reverent and attentive energy. If these two energies overlap, it could feel conflicting. Instead of fully relaxing, you may feel judged or restrained, especially if you wish to do naughty things. This only applies to altars dedicated to deities or ancestors. Subtle spiritual objects to provide calm, such as crystals or art, are okay.

**Fix it!**

Place altars and shrines where their sacred energy feels respected.

- Choose a higher-energy communal area, such as the living or dining area, which are active spaces already, but don't block with furniture or clutter.
- If you prefer somewhere calmer, quiet spaces such as study rooms or home offices are good – the shrine can even support you as you work.
- Avoid placing altars close to 'unclean' places such as toilets or neglected spaces, like under staircases.

Feng shui itself is non-religious. The following notes are general guidelines only; further reading is recommended. Overall, the key is to understand the meaning behind each practice and apply it thoughtfully in your home:

– East Asian traditions (Buddhist or Taoist): Shrines are often placed facing the general direction of the entrance, receiving the energy of the outside.
– Vastu Shastra: The north-east corner of the home is considered the most suitable for a pooja (a Hindu ritual).
– Christian traditions: A cross over the bed is seen as a symbol of quiet protection, and is acceptable in the bedroom.
– Islam: Prayer is oriented towards the Kaaba, and it is acceptable to pray in the bedroom.
– Judaism: A mezuzah is usually placed on the outside of the doorframe to bless the transition into the room rather than in the room itself.

# FURNITURE,

# LIGHTS

# AND FIXTURES

46

# My bed doesn't need a headboard, it's just decoration anyway

**Rating:**

Feng shui says... sleeping without a headboard will weaken your support in life.

**Why**

When we sleep, we want to feel supported and even embraced. A headboard provides this where it matters most, close to our head, giving a sense of security and protection. In feng shui, we see this like the mountain supporting us from behind. Practically, a headboard allows you to lean back when you are sitting in bed, and means that you won't feel as though you're floating in space while sleeping. It's a little like how a chair with a backrest feels more comfortable than a stool. Over time, sleeping without a headrest can subtly affect your sleep and, in turn, your mind.

**Fix it!**

Get a bed with a headboard! There is no reason not to have one.

- If your bed is against a window, a headboard is even more important, so choose a strong, solid one. In addition, hang curtains to block out the window when you sleep.
- If your bed is pushed into the corner of the room, and a headboard looks strange on its own, get a bed with a head, side and footboard, so it creates a cocoon.
- Add a feature on the wall. If your bed does not come with a headboard, attach a padded panel to the wall; even a piece of painted wood can work.
- Paint one. If you don't want a headboard or there is no space, you can paint a fake headboard, or even paint the entire wall behind the bed a darker colour to represent this support. Glossier paint helps it stay clean.
- Add pillows. If your headboard is particularly low or lacks support, add cushions or pillows to compensate.

47

# My bed is a queen and my roommate's is a single, he says it's not fair

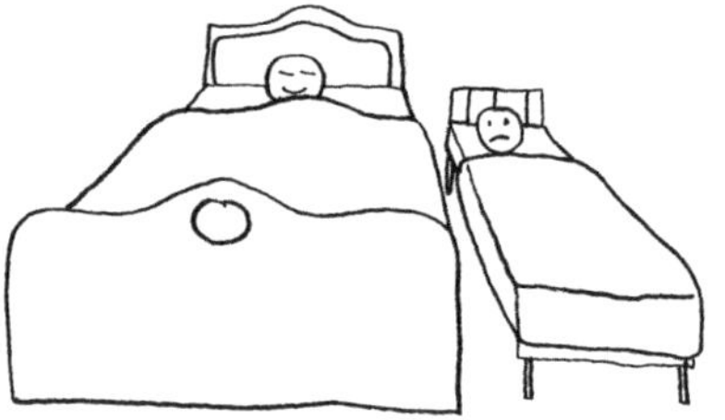

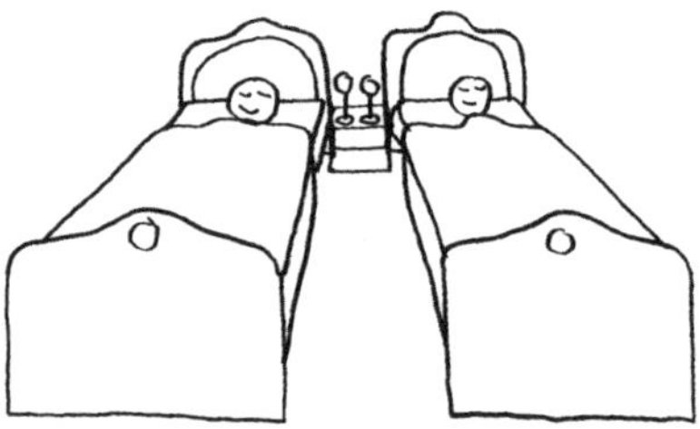

**Rating:**

Feng shui says... if you have different-sized beds in the same room, one of you will feel bullied by the other.

### Why

In feng shui, a bed is a mirror of the person sleeping in it. When a room has beds of different sizes, it means that one is more dominant than the other. Cultural meanings aside, a bigger bed represents more space, comfort and dominance, while the smaller bed represents limitation and compromise. If the room is shared between siblings, this can symbolise unfairness and favouritism. If it is shared between a couple, it shows that one of the partners is 'giving in' to the other. While making compromises for your loved one might be a noble gesture, over time, you will eventually feel the imbalance, which might affect your relationship.

### Fix it!

If you need two beds in the same room, make them as similar as possible.

- Choose two identical beds. It's important, especially for siblings sharing a room, that these beds are the same size and appearance, so that everyone feels like they have a fair amount of space.
- If you need to have different-sized beds, make sure the relationship is clear. For example, if you need to share a room with your child, use a very kiddy-looking bed for them and a larger one for yourself, to emphasise your relationship dynamic (a baby cot in the bedroom is fine).
- Avoid pairing a double and a single bed in a couple's room, as this symbolises a third person entering the relationship.
- Add a daybed or sofabed in the bedroom. If you need to sleep separately for cultural reasons, then the spare bed will not feel like a bed when not in use.
- Have two separate beds. If you find that you and your partner actually prefer to sleep separately, then feel free to get two smaller beds, but keep two side tables and table lamps (not four) to remind you of your unity.

# Our bed is made of two mattresses and I keep falling into the gap

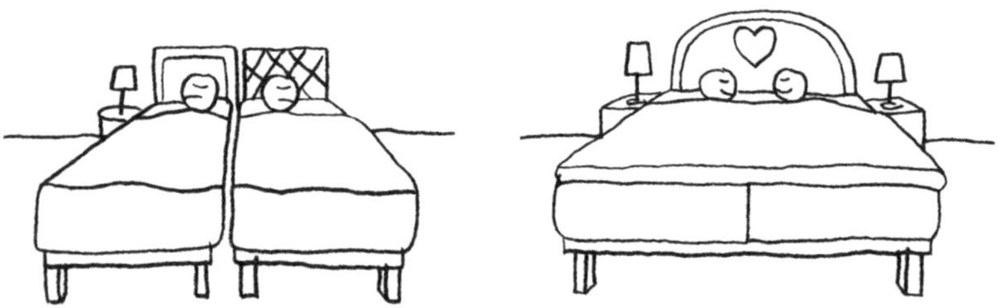

**Rating:** 

Feng shui says... if you share a bed with your partner, a gap within it represents a hidden rift, leading to separation.

**Why**

When a bed shared between a couple is split down the middle, whether it is made of two mattresses or two separate beds put side by side, it represents a hidden divide. This may sound far-fetched, but in feng shui, the bed is one of the strongest symbols of matrimony and even fertility. Practically, couples may have a reason to sleep on separate mattresses, be it comfort or cultural, and it really shouldn't affect their relationship that much. However, when the separation is obvious, for example one mattress is thicker than the other, or the gap is big enough that you constantly lose your phone or leg in it, then the separation is obvious, and may remind you that your partner is really nothing more than your housemate.

**Fix it!**

You ideally don't want to be able to tell that the beds are separate and should minimise the gap as much as you can.

- If possible, sleep on the same mattress. Choose one that's larger, so the space between you gives a sense of independence, without losing the effect of unity. Or choose a unified mattress that can absorb movement. Pocket-sprung mattresses for example, can distribute weight separately, so you would not feel your partner tossing and turning.
- If your mattresses need to remain separate, ensure that something is connected. For example, choose one bedframe that fits the two separate mattresses. Whatever else you do, ensure that the design of the headboard is a single continuous piece.
- Use a mattress topper to make the beds feel like one, at least from the top, and a single duvet or blanket, so that you are wrapped up together at night.
- Ensure the two mattresses are the same thickness and appearance. This is so there will be no height difference.
- Have two side tables and table lamps (ideally with mattresses pushed together) to remind you of your unity.

# I want to put my kids in bunk beds, but they are fighting to get the top

**Rating:** 

Feng shui says... children sleeping on bunk beds will suffer from uneven luck and restlessness.

**Why**

Bunk beds mean that one child will be above and the other below. This immediately creates imbalance. In feng shui terms, the kid on top will receive an excess of energy, making them feel active, highly charged and even reckless and prone to accidents, while the one below will feel stifled, suppressed and pushed down, perhaps even having their luck taken away. These feelings might sound trivial, or even superstitious, but practically speaking, bunk beds do affect lifestyle: the child in the top bunk will not have access to their things and the child in the lower bunk will always feel the movement of the one above. Both children will lose a sense of their own space. They will never feel fully independent and their sleep will be affected too.

**Fix it!**

Give as much autonomous space to each person as possible.

- Have two separate beds, even if it means that the beds are very close together or even touching. It's okay for the short ends of the beds to touch, but don't pair them up side by side like a big double bed.
- Avoid desk beds. Bunk beds are still better than beds with a desk below, because it is worse to try to work under a bed than to sleep under it.
- Place the older child above. This suggests the natural hierarchy, where the older child gets opportunities first while protecting the younger one. Since the older one will leave sooner, the younger kid will get their chance to have space later.
- Decorate each level of the bed so they feel more independent and add soft, diffused lighting to the lower bunk to reduce the feeling of being pressed down.

# My dining table is not a circle, does it matter?

**Rating:** 

Feng shui says... irregularly shaped tables may create imbalance in your family harmony.

**Why**

The dining room is often the heart of the home, where the family gathers and connects. Because of this, the shape of your dining table can play a subtle but important role. In feng shui, we prefer round tables because they symbolise harmony and wholeness: no sharp corners, no head of the table and everyone has equal access to one another. That said, rectangular tables are perfectly acceptable too. However, things get trickier with irregularly shaped dining tables, such as trapezoidal, triangular or organic shapes. Not because they look strange, but because some shapes may force members of the family to sit further out, making them feel left out or cut off, and that is something that can slowly affect family dynamics over time.

**Fix it!**

Choose a dining table that allows everyone to feel included.

- Round tables encourage balance and equality. They work best for four to six people; if the table is too large, it will be harder to hold a conversation. Choose one with a pedestal base if possible, as that's more flexible.
- Rectangular tables are the most versatile. Smaller groups can use the end of the table with nobody feeling left out. Though it's worth noting that people on the ends might receive more or less energy, creating a sense of hierarchy. Even if your table is a normal rectangle, avoid sitting at the corner where it pokes at you.
- Square tables tend to limit the number of people to four, which may feel restrictive if you want to host more.
- If you love your irregular table and must have it, ensure that nobody feels left out. Avoid shapes with sharp angles, missing corners or uneven sides. Before buying it, try to sit at various parts of the table to see if any seat feels less connected.
- If you are joining tables for a larger group, keep shapes simple. It is better to have two separate groups rather than a strange 'L' shape configuration where people can be 'trapped' in corners.

51

# Our dining table is clear glass and it's weird to see everyone's feet

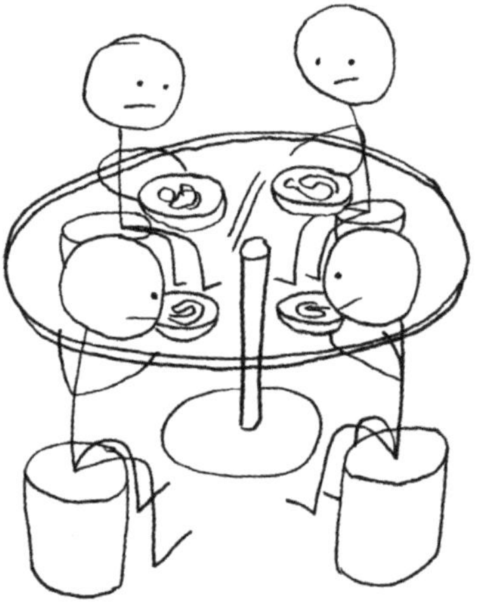

**Rating:**

Feng shui says... having a clear-glass dining table means that your family ties will be unstable and fragile.

## Why

A dining table is a symbol of togetherness and family, and feng shui prefers solid, stable materials for this platform, like wood or stone. These are both very grounding materials which symbolise the earth element, meaning unity and strength. But a glass table, with its transparency and reflectivity, is seen as fragile and weak. Practically speaking, a clear glass table leads everyone to look at each other's feet, rather than their faces.

## Fix it!

It is less about the material and more about the sense of stability and grounding.

- Put a tablecloth over it to create a sense of weight and stability. You only have to do this when you're hosting.
- Use placemats if you find tablecloths too formal. They create little pockets of stability for each person at the table.
- Hang a statement chandelier over the table. While the table may be weak, the chandelier will act as a magnet to draw everyone together, albeit upwards.
- Place a grounding centrepiece in the middle of the table, like a terracotta vase or bowl with fruit or flowers inside (a good idea for prosperity regardless of your table material, see page 168).
- Choose thick or opaque glass. It is less about the material and more about the feeling. Remember, choose a material that feels solid and grounding, as opposed to thin and fragile.
- It is perfectly acceptable to have glass on your dining table. For example, if you have a wooden table with a glass topper, or a stone table that is polished so it's shiny like glass.

# My dining table has an odd number of chairs, should I take one away?

**Rating:**

Feng shui says... when the numbers don't pair up, you invite unwanted guests to the table!

### Why

In feng shui, we prefer pairs and even numbers because it means that everyone has a companion. But when there are odd numbers, someone is likely to be left out. It's similar to when you hang out with your friends in a couple, and they are kissing while you awkwardly look at them. Plus it just looks more balanced to have an equal number of chairs on both sides. Don't panic though, you can absolutely have an odd number of people at the table – but the number of chairs, which is considered a long-term decision, should be even. The superstition is that if there is an odd chair hanging around, it means that you are intentionally inviting a single person, unwanted guests or even ghosts to join!

### Fix it!

Have even number of chairs at the table (unless there is a strong reason for an uneven number, like your table is a triangle).

- Stick to even numbers. Regardless of table shape, aim for an even number of chairs: two, four, six. Try not to have a triangular-shaped table, as this will make it hard to have an even number of chairs.

- A bench can represent two or more seats. If your room is asymmetrical and it does not make sense to have four chairs, you may replace some chairs with a bench. This way the unevenness is less obvious.

- Put spare chairs in storage. Do not leave them in the room leaning against walls as this also suggests people being left out.

- Baby chairs are fine because a baby is considered a new addition during their early years. Once the child is older, give them a proper chair (make sure the chairs are an even number!) so the table feels comfortably balanced again.

53

# There are slatted blinds on my window, it's like an interrogation room

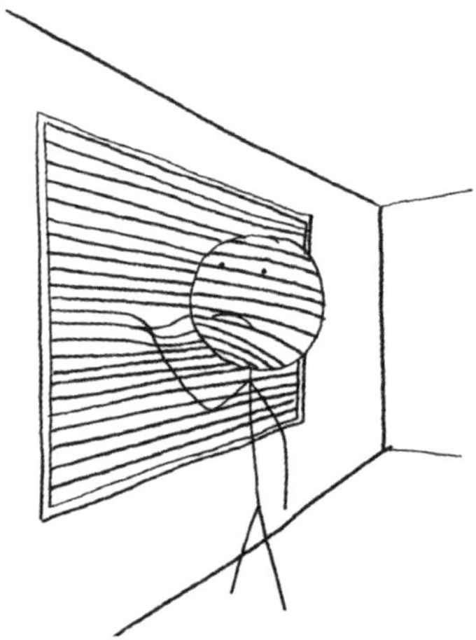

**Rating:**

Feng shui says... slatted blinds such as Venetian blinds will create feelings of tension in the home.

**Why**

Windows are a source of natural light and life-giving energy. When you use blinds that are made of individual slats, you break this energy into harsh strips of intermittent light and shadow. Because the light enters in broken bars, your eyes struggle to adjust, causing visual strain, and the room can start to feel tense and uncomfortable, like an interrogation room. Over time, you will avoid looking at the windows completely and they become a mental fence between you and the outside world, making your home feel like a prison. Of course, another practical problem with slatted blinds is that they are hard to keep clean.

**Fix it!**

Natural light should come through windows in a soft, comfortable way.

- Avoid slatted blinds altogether: opt for curtains to give softness or, if you prefer modern, clean lines, use roller blinds or Roman blinds.
- Try alternatives like honeycomb blinds, which are versatile and easily controlled, while not actually slicing your view.
- Avoid vertical lines. Vertical slats are worse than horizontal as their lines make your room feel even more like a prison.
- Layer with curtains. If you cannot remove your slatted blinds, you may soften the look by layering curtains over them.
- Avoid striped roller blinds. These blinds, which alternate opaque and translucent strips, create as much visual tension as Venetian blinds, so are best avoided too.

# My industrial lightbulbs are so cool, I feel like I'm in a cafe – but I can't sleep

**Rating:** 

Feng shui says... exposed lightbulbs can cause tension and stress.

**Why**

Lighting has a powerful effect on how we feel in a space. A naked bulb with a visible filament gives off a harsh, piercing glare that is aggressive and hard on the eyes. Over time, this kind of lighting will make your room feel uncomfortable, even confrontational, like an interrogation room. Such harsh lighting is overly yang, and can be draining when overused. The best type of lighting is shaded or diffused to give a softer, more calming glow. The colour temperature of your bulb can also affect your senses. Warmer colour temperatures such as 2700–3000K are best for living and resting spaces, while cooler temperatures like 4000K and above are overly white and best for workspaces or hospitals.

**Fix it!**

It depends on the look you want in your space, but remember, lighting is supposed to give comfort.

- Diffuse the light. Use a lampshade or paper shade to soften the glare from the lightbulb to create a gentler glow.
- Lower the intensity. If you want the industrial look of a naked bulb, choose a lower wattage so it is less blinding for the eye. Treat this as decorative lighting rather than the main source of light.
- Distribute the light. Instead of a single strong bulb, use multiple smaller ones so the lighting is sparkling but not glaring. Still, such dazzling lighting should only be used in communal spaces like dining or living rooms, not the bedroom.
- Use multiple sources of light. Think table lamps and floor lamps dotted around the home instead of relying on exposed bulbs as central light sources.

55

# My lightbulbs are flickering, but I'll deal with them later

**Rating:**

Feng shui says... flickering bulbs in the home can weaken mental clarity and cause instability.

**Why**

Anything broken is generally considered inauspicious in feng shui, but objects we interact with daily are the most disruptive when left unfixed. Flickering bulbs, squeaky doors or leaky taps are not just inconveniences, they affect the flow of our daily lives and gradually our mental state. Bulbs are particularly important. When light is unstable, our eyes are forced to constantly adjust, creating visual stress and mental fatigue. It also sends an unconscious distress signal, like you're in a haunted room. Squeaky hinges mean we become unnecessarily cautious when opening and closing the doors, and leaky taps waste precious water, which is symbolic of wealth leaking out of our homes.

**Fix it!**

When something is used on a daily basis, don't live with the problem, fix it as soon as possible and you will thank yourself later (or immediately).

- Replace flickering bulbs immediately. It might seem minor, but the effect of something broken or not working as it should accumulates over time.
- Check for safety. Flickering lights might be a sign of loose connections, so take it as a sign to check and make your home safe.

For anything else broken:

- Lubricate any squeaky joints; it's so easy to do and makes a big difference.
- Fix leaky taps, shower heads, or anything that has water in it. Uncontrolled water can lead to mould or damp issues, and symbolises loss of wealth.
- Repair all other broken things, like loose hinges, dangling hooks or ripped curtains. Often, small annoyances are disproportionally easier to fix than the frustration that they cause over extended periods of time.

56

# There is a big chandelier hanging over me, I hope it does not drop

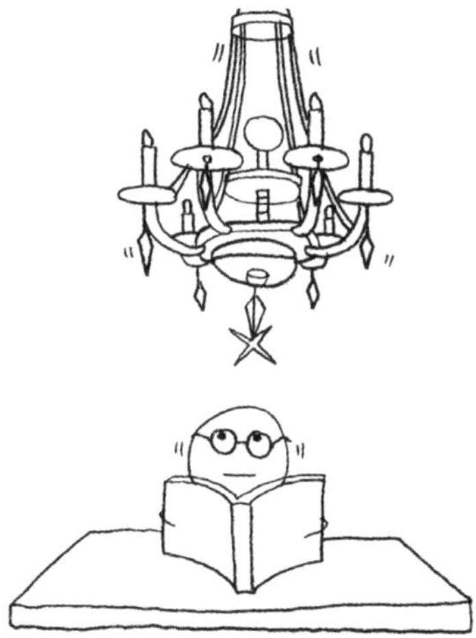

**Rating:**

Feng shui says... a large, heavy chandelier hanging directly over you causes feelings of pressure and anxiety.

**Why**

In feng shui, anything big and heavy hanging directly over you is considered to have sha chi or 'killing energy'. Imagine a big, heavy chandelier dangling precariously above you, along with its hundreds of crystal shards, all held up by just a single chain. Even though we know that it is not going to fall, its presence alone is enough to make us feel uneasy and even anxious, which affects our ability to relax or focus. Safety aside, a big chandelier also has a commanding energy which draws all eyes towards it, and in turn towards you, seated directly below. This energy can be good in the right context, for instance regulating the fiercely whizzing energy around an entry foyer, or to anchor the centre of a dining room, but it should never hang above a person.

**Fix it!**

Make the most of the commanding weight of a chandelier and hang it in the right place.

- Consider the ceiling height. Chandeliers work best in rooms with higher ceilings. In lower spaces they can feel overwhelming, so consider wall sconces or indirect lighting like floor and table lamps instead.
- Anchor it to furniture. Hang chandeliers over dining tables or coffee tables so no one can walk or sit directly beneath them. This also allows you to hang them slightly lower without it looking wrong.
- Avoid sitting underneath a chandelier, not matter what. Even in tall rooms, avoid placing your sofa, desk or bed directly under a chandelier.
- Always centre it. Because of a chandelier's imposing presence, it should always be centred to something, be it the centre of the room or the centre of the dining table.
- Choose something lighter! If you want to hang a light over your bed, choose a lighter, fluffier object like a paper pendant, rather than a heavy crystal fixture.

# There's a big ceiling fan over me, it's so windy

**Rating:** 

Feng shui says... a big fan spinning above you will create cutting energy and cause you to feel restless.

### Why

A big ceiling fan is considered inauspicious for two reasons. One: it's a giant blade spinning dangerously above you. This naturally creates a sense of anxiety and nervousness. Two: it forces a downward pressure of air, which is quite unnatural. This actually causes you to feel suppressed and disturbs the calm energy of your room. The energy is especially bad if you are directly below the fan, for example if your couch is in the middle of the room with the fan above you, or if it's right above your bed. But the worst is if it's over the bed, whirling all night long, as this is a constant and active energy bombarding you – like trying to sleep in a hurricane.

### Fix it!

Minimise the energy coming from above as much as you can.

- Consider alternatives to ceiling fans, such as standing or table-top fans. This way, you still enjoy the air circulation without the precarious energy looming above you.
- Bladeless options. There are modern bladeless ceiling fans which look discreet and calm, while still offering the same kind of circulation.
- Reduce the speed. If you do have a ceiling fan, turn it to the lowest setting, so the movement is slow and gentle. This will feel less like a wind turbine in a factory.
- Reposition yourself. Avoid placing beds or sofas directly under the fan. In bedrooms, the fan could be above the foot of the bed and in living rooms, above the coffee table, so you never run the risk of being under it.
- Protect yourself. In bedrooms, consider canopy beds to give a thin layer of visual protection to soften the fan's energy.

# I love the look of a wall of shelves, and they're great for storage

**Rating:** 

Feng shui says... a big wall of open shelves can create unease and scattered feelings.

**Why**

In feng shui, exposed shelves, with their sharp, open edges, are often compared to blades that give off sha chi or 'killing energy'. This is because their protruding forms can feel aggressive. In addition, if placed poorly – especially at head height or with sharp corners – they can pose an actual risk, where you could bump your head or poke your eyes out. In addition, open shelves mean openly displayed items. While there is nothing wrong with a beautifully curated shelf, when shelves are untidy or overloaded (this particularly happens when used for storage) they can be visually unstable and chaotic. This brings clutter to your eye level, or worse, above you. Over time, the constant visual noise might remind us of how disorganised and chaotic our own lives are, making us feel overwhelmed and stressed.

**Fix it!**

Limit the amount of open shelving and use closed storage (add cabinet doors!), or keep them always looking pretty.

- Keep open shelving curated and organised. Reserve these for decorative things or books. When it comes to books, always place them vertically, spine out.
- Use boxes or baskets. If your shelves must function as storage, keep smaller items inside boxes. Place these on the lower levels with the shelves above still reserved for decorative items. If hiding your things makes you forget they exist, add labels to the boxes to remind yourself.
- Avoid open shelves above where you sit or rest. Nothing over your desk, your bed or behind your couch, especially if it actually hangs over you.
- Keep shelves clean and dusted. If the shelves look neglected, they will create the same sense of visual weight.

DECOR ITEMS

AND

THINGS

59

# I love this cracked mirror design, but it looks wrong

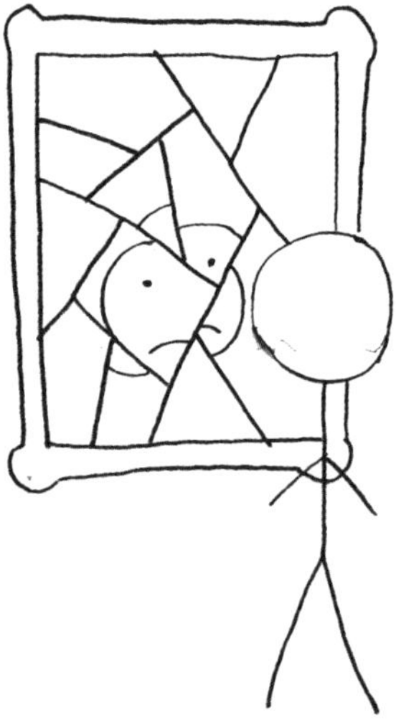

**Rating:** 

Feng shui says... a broken mirror means a fractured self-image and bad luck.

**Why**

Mirrors have long been seen as mystical things that capture entire worlds within them. They represent clarity, truth and reality. Looking into a mirror is the main way we see ourselves, and it's a powerful window to self-reflection and recognition. When this reflection is broken, our own self-image becomes incomplete, torn or even mutilated. While we know practically that it is just a reflection, seeing your face split in two or your head detached from your body will psychologically create subconscious triggers, slowly affecting our confidence, clarity and inner balance.

**Fix it!**

Avoid broken mirrors entirely, or avoid seeing them as much as possible.

- Do not keep any broken mirrors, and if your existing mirrors break, dispose of them immediately.
- Hide the parts that are cracked with plants or flowers, decorate them with embellishments or covers, or even use repair techniques like kintsugi to make it look intentional. Note that this can only work for mirrors with minor damage and only if the main central reflection is unaffected.
- Never allow yourself to see a broken reflection. If your mirror is designed such that it will always create a fragmented reflection, hang it so that it is impossible to catch your own reflection in it.
- Distorted or antique mirrors where reflections are not clear should also be avoided.

# I have a huge mirror in front of my bed, it's so sexy but I can't sleep

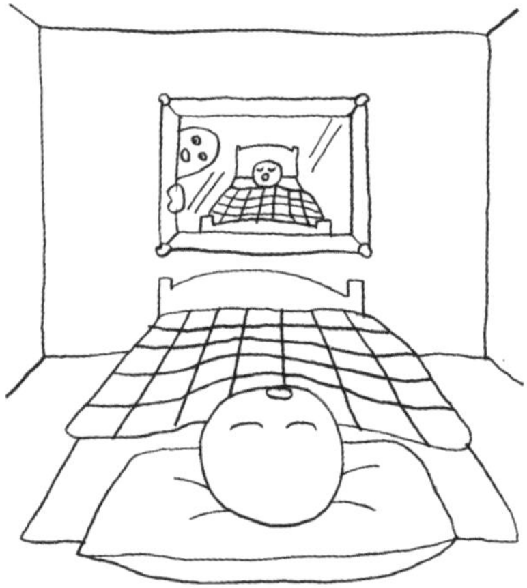

**Rating:** 

Feng shui says... a mirror right in front of you can become a portal for spirits to enter your room, or for your own to escape!

**Why**

We all know that mirrors double whatever's reflected in them, but when the lights are switched off, they take on a special quality. In the darkness of night, mirrors appear more like windows or doors. They reflect motion and movement and draw your attention to them. When you are sleepy, you might mistake your own shadowy reflection for an intruder, which will startle you. Mirrors, which are also used for security, can give the impression that you are being surveyed or watched. Even when you're not in bed, having a mirror facing you when you work or eat may bring about too much self-awareness, making you think and worry about your appearance. It's an unnecessary distraction. Don't worry if your hotel room has a big mirror in front of the bed – it's only for a night, and sometimes people want that kind of excitement when they are on holiday.

**Fix it!**

Your personal reflection should only be seen when sought – never unintentionally.

- Avoid mirrors in front of your bed, or in any position where you can see yourself while sleeping. The best places for a mirror are in the hallway area of your room, or perpendicular to the bed, but closer to the foot, so you don't see yourself if you sleep sideways.
- If there is a mirror in front of you, cover it with fabric when not in use. This also applies to televisions with their glossy black surfaces.
- Angle the mirror so it does not point straight at you. You shouldn't be able to see yourself in the mirror, and the reflection shouldn't be busy.
- Stick on a frosted overlay or use a curtain. This is useful if you have a wall of mirrors as your wardrobe doors.
- Avoid mirrors facing you in general. This applies to having mirrors in front of your desk, sofa and particularly in the kitchen, as mirrors can amplify the already high energy, and make you think you are cooking yourself.

# Can I put a mirror at the end of the hallway to make it look bigger?

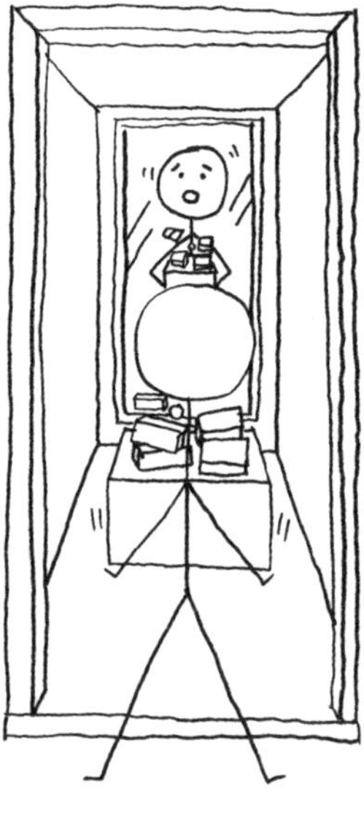

**Rating:** 

Feng shui says... mirrors at the end of hallways will cause your energy to bounce and flutter.

## Why

Hallways are busy circulation routes and they carry a lot of movement and energy. At the same time, mirrors reflect and amplify whatever is in front of them. When a mirror is placed at the end of a hallway, it creates a sensation of you walking towards yourself. This can feel confrontational or startling, as if the space is ejecting you rather than welcoming you in. The same effect happens when you have a mirror facing a door. Every time you enter, you are met with your own reflection, which can feel like a visual pushback. This is why in feng shui, a mirror facing the front door is especially bad, because the front door is where opportunities and fortune enter your home, so the mirror symbolically reflects all these nice things back out the door. Staircases work similarly: a mirror at the top or bottom of a staircase will create a sense of imbalance while you move up or down it. Mirrors should, therefore, not be placed where movement is meant to continue forward.

## Fix it!

Avoid mirrors at the end of circulation paths or facing doors or stairs.

- Use artwork instead. If the wall feels empty, hang artwork, as this will create more depth and interest than a mirror.
- Place mirrors on the side walls. Mirrors are absolutely fine in hallways, as long as they don't face you. Position them on the sides, and they will even make the hallway feel wider.
- Anchor the mirror. If you really want a mirror at the end of your hallway or in front of your door, put something with it, like a side table or a flourishing plant, to signify that the hallway ends.
- Avoid mirrors facing entryways. As a general rule, mirrors should not directly face doors. Bathrooms are an exception, as mirrors are expected there and these rooms rarely disrupt the main flow of the home.

62

# There is a big mirror hanging behind me, are you using it to spy on me?

**Rating:**

Feng shui says... hanging a large mirror behind you will make you vulnerable to surprise attacks.

**Why**

A mirror is like a window into yourself. Normally, you present yourself in a certain way to others, controlling what they see. But when there is a mirror hanging behind you, it can reflect parts that you never intended to show – your unguarded self. You'll feel exposed and vulnerable, as if other people looking at the mirror can peek into your private self. This can affect you in different ways, depending on the context. For example, if the mirror is behind your desk, people can see your computer screen and what you are working on. If it's hanging behind the couch, intimate conversations might feel less private. If it's hanging above your bed, it will feel like your bed is not grounded. Also, mirrors are heavy, so hanging them above you might feel dangerous!

**Fix it!**

Be mindful of where you hang mirrors and use them only where appropriate.

- Reposition mirrors. Evaluate your surroundings and hang mirrors so that they do not reflect you in ways you don't intend. Since mirrors double everything in their path, hang them so that they reflect only positive and beautiful things.

- Choose alternatives. If you have a big empty wall, you can hang artwork or panelling instead of mirrors. If the wall is behind your desk, it will be your backdrop, so choose something that you want to be associated with.

- Make it part of a gallery wall. Smaller mirrors that form part of a larger gallery wall composition are fine, as the mirror is no longer the focal point.

- Be careful with decorative mirrors like frosted or faceted mirrors. Although they obscure reflections, they also distort them, which is another feng shui no-no.

63

# I have an expensive broken teacup I love and I can’t bear to throw it away

**Rating:** 

Feng shui says... hanging onto broken things blocks new opportunities and growth.

**Why**

Keeping broken items in the home is considered inauspicious not just because they look bad, but because they block fresh energy and opportunities from entering our lives. This stems from the idea that if we cannot let go, we are not ready for change or to move forward. This is especially true for objects that can no longer serve their purpose, like a favourite teacup that is cracked so you can't drink from it anymore. Sentimental or monetary attachment can make it hard to let go of these items, but keeping them has an emotional cost. They remind us of loss, our clumsiness, or can even send a false signal that we cannot afford to replace them, reinforcing the sense of struggle.

**Fix it!**

While we should not be wasteful, avoid keeping things that prevent you from moving forward.

- Dispose of it. If something is broken beyond use, release it immediately. Especially if it no longer serves a function, like a cup or vase.
- Repair it. If the item is worth fixing or repairing, do so as soon as possible to bring it back to use, or store it away in the meantime.
- Transform it. Repurpose it into something new or artistic. Kintsugi, the Japanese art of renewal, is a good example of turning flaws into beauty.
- Hide the damage. If you must keep and display the broken object, position it so the break is hidden from view.
- Honour and release. For sentimental items that cannot be salvaged, thank it for its service and dispose of it respectfully. Holding onto it will only cause more sadness.

64

# I’m too lazy to keep my kitchen knives away, is it okay to leave them out?

**Rating:** 

Feng shui says... displaying big sharp knives in your home will cause tension, leading to arguments and quarrels.

### Why

Knives are aggressive objects. They are essentially weapons on show and remind us of their potential for harm. Having knives on display in the kitchen, or anywhere else in the home for that matter, creates uncontrollable associations with violence, which leads to subconscious feelings of aggression, sharp tension and even conflict. This applies to all types of sharp blade-like objects: scissors, craft knives, ceremonial swords. Even if you like the look of knives on display, their sharp angles can create a heightened sense of alertness, which disturbs the calm in your space.

### Fix it!

Knives and weapon-like objects should be kept safely and, ideally, out of sight.

- The more intimate and yin a space is, the stronger the negative impact of exposed knives. Avoid knives or sharp objects in the bedroom, living areas or other calm spaces. It may be acceptable in workshops, training rooms or specialised kitchens, where the knife or display weapon needs to be located conveniently.

- Store knives properly. Keep them in cutlery drawers or inside cabinets, and only pull them out when you need to use them. Imagine you have little kids when you're planning the position of the knives: you wouldn't want the kids to get too curious about the knives, so store them away.

- Never aim the blade outwards. If knives have to be visible – for example, if you need them within easy reach – place them blade down, like in a knife block, so only the handles are exposed. Avoid magnetic knife holders.

- Display knives safely. If you need/want to display knives or swords, place them inside display cabinets, and point them away from where people typically gather.

# I love cacti and want them all over my house

**Rating:** 

Feng shui says... a cactus, with its sharp prickles, can lead to defensive energy and loneliness.

**Why**

The sharp, pointy appearance of cacti generally gives off a hostile and defensive energy, similar to displaying swords or rifles in your home. While they might scare off intruders, having these aggressive objects in the wrong place, like a bedroom, can disrupt the energy and make your calm room feel awake and restless. It's not just about cacti; any plant that looks sharp and aggressive, like a snake plant, should be placed away from calm spaces.

**Fix it!**

The key is to choose plants that reflect the feelings that you want in the space, based on their general appearance and leaf shape.

- Cacti, snake plants, yucca and other spiky plants represent protection and are used to ward off evil. They are best located in windows or close to entrances. Ideally, keep them away from where you sleep or relax, but if you want to have them in those spaces, use rounded or curvy pots to soften their sharp energy.
- Succulents are related to cacti, but if they have cute roundish leaves, they are acceptable anywhere in the home.
- Rubber plants, monstera, ZZ plants, fig trees and other plants with roundish leaves are better because their softly rounded and richly coloured leaves represent fullness and abundance and can be placed anywhere in the house (though limit any kinds of plants in sleeping areas).
- Spider plants, palms and ferns have spiky shapes but their leaves are soft, so these, too, are acceptable in the home. As they have a more energetic appearance, they are better suited to living spaces.
- Jade plants or Chinese money plants have cute round leaves that are shaped like coins, and are perfect for the money corner. Although any plant can go here because a plant's main symbolism is growth.
- Most importantly, keep your plants healthy and green! A happy, healthy plant – regardless of type – is always better than a sad-looking one.

66

# All my plants are dead, I feel like giving up

**Rating:**

Feng shui says... dead plants represent a decaying and withering home, weakening your vitality.

### Why

We generally try to avoid dead things in feng shui (this is different from motifs of death, which can be intentional). Dead plants are the consequence of unintentional neglect or even deprivation. Having these in our home would subtly remind us of our failure to keep something alive, or suggest the home itself is lacking nourishment and vitality. While it's obvious dead plants are bad, a more contentious example is dried plants. These are often displayed for their aesthetic appeal, they have subtle connotations behind them. For example, fluffy dried plumes could remind us of the dryness of a desert, or bare twigs the bitter cold of winter, both of which are not environments that we associate with comfort and warmth.

### Fix it!

Avoid dead plants entirely! Remove them and replace them with objects of similar visual weight without the emotional baggage.

- Dispose of any plants that have died. It sounds like common sense, but many of us start with fresh plants that slowly die without us even noticing. Take a walk around your home and look out for any plants which are gone or on the brink of death. If you can save it, do so, but if it is beyond redemption, end its pain.
- If you must have dried plants, choose vibrant colours. Examples are dried hydrangeas or preserved flowers which still have a fullness and life to them.
- Replace dried plants with other similarly shaped objects. A good example is large vibrant feathers in a vase, or even decorative items with the fullness and volume of plants, such as sculptures or lamps.

67

# It’s Halloween and I want to decorate my home with skulls

**Rating:** 

Feng shui says... motifs of death in the house are inauspicious and drain your life energy.

## Why

There are two sides of feng shui, one for the living and one for the dead. They are not meant to be mixed. Feng shui for the living – the type that this book is about – encourages the notion of sheng chi, or life energy. Images of death, such as skulls or dead animals, are overly yin, and evoke feelings of loss and endings. Practically, these might lead us to ponder our mortality a little too much, dampening motivation, vitality or passion. This is not only about skulls, though; anything that has connections with death, even flowers such as lilies or white chrysanthemums, or animal trophies, like deer heads with their sparkly eyes staring sadly at you, can carry emotional weight.

## Fix it!

Be conscious of what you display, and only have objects that make you feel the way you want to feel.

- Make a distinction between festive decoration and genuine interest. Decorating with skulls and ghosts for Halloween is fine, as long as you know it's all for fun.
- Understand your interest. If you want to display death motifs as a serious part of your decor, ask yourself: what is it that you enjoy about these motifs? If you appreciate the life-giving nature of death and see something positive in the motifs, then it is actually fine to have them on display. However, if they make you feel sad and melancholy, consider limiting them.
- Choose locations that fit the skull's energy, like rooms with reflective and contemplative energy, such as offices or libraries. Avoid them in bedrooms, dining rooms or kitchens.
- It's not only about death. Some decorations, even festive ones like nutcracker dolls at Christmas, can occasionally evoke unsettling energy, and should be avoided in bedrooms. In a nutshell (mind the pun), anything you display can carry visual weight, and should be put out thoughtfully.

# I need to hide the presents that my ex gave me from my dates

**Rating:** 

Feng shui says... memories of old relationships lying around will prevent you from making new ones.

**Why**

Everything that you have at home carries some kind of energy. Items that remind you of past relationships, events or emotions can affect how you feel and influence your behaviour. For example, being surrounded by gifts from your ex-partner could make you long for the past, or fear for the future. Either way, these inanimate objects might evoke very real emotions. Your home should support your growth and wellbeing, and it is important to curate what you have on show so that you will feel energised rather than drained.

**Fix it!**

Be surrounded by things that give you positive or uplifting feelings.

- Get rid of things that drag you down. Anything that triggers bad memories, regret or pain should be removed right away.
- Store things. If you have something that holds sentimental value which gives you sadness – for example something from a loved one who has passed away – keep it safe in a precious box, but out of sight, so it does not influence your daily energy.
- Be selective of where things go. Some keepsakes are fine, but their location matters. A memento of a loved one who has passed might feel sad in a private space like the bedroom, but it can feel comforting in a shared area, like the living room, where they can be remembered with friends and family.
- Lighten its energy. If you have a gift from an ex that gives you happy feelings, mix it up with gifts from other people, such as friends or family. This prevents us from focusing on the failed relationship and reframes the gifts as a collective.
- Transform the energy. For items that are very expensive, try to sell them and use the money to get yourself something that makes you happy. If you are unable to sell the item or if you like it but not its memory, consider repurposing or altering it in some way. This allows you to release its past association and refresh the energy.

69

# My cat's litter box is in my bedroom, which is practical but smelly

**Rating:**

Feng shui says... A litter box can pollute your room and affect your wellbeing.

**Why**

A litter box is a modern invention. Ancient Chinese people would not generally let their animals poop inside their inner chambers, so there is no direct feng shui rule at play here. However, any form of waste is considered disruptive because the smells or visual associations can trigger feelings of aversion, unease or even danger. When these cues are present in important places such as your living, eating or resting rooms, they can cause you to have resentment towards your home and even your pet. Even if you don't mind smelling your cat or rabbit's poop, your pet might consider your room a latrine area, which is something even wild animals don't like to spend time in. Smells aside, the sound of your cat digging at night can also be disruptive.

**Fix it!**

The litter box should be as discreet and hidden as possible, both visually and aromatically.

- Choose the right location. Place litter boxes in support areas such as utility rooms, boot rooms or storage areas. Bathrooms and closets work, as long as pets can access them though a pet door or flap. Avoid living areas, dining areas, entrances and bedrooms. If it needs to be in one of these rooms, find a spot within it that is far from where you sleep, sit or eat.
- Avoid the money corner. In feng shui, there are special parts of the home which are more visible and visually important, such as the money corner, which should only contain auspicious objects, so don't place the litter box there.
- Be thoughtful about where you hide it. Open litter boxes are sometimes better for your pet, so if you decide to have an exposed placement, put plants around it. Even fake plants are fine in this instance.
- Keep it clean and fresh. Most importantly, keep the litter box clean by removing the little poops promptly. You might also add charcoal or baking soda to absorb smells.

# I like to decorate with plastic plants

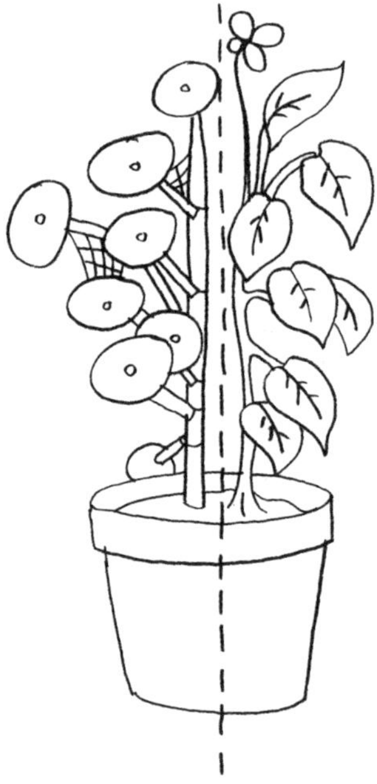

**Rating:** 

Feng shui says... fake plants mean fake prosperity, and you will stop growing, like a plastic plant.

**Why**

In feng shui, a plant represents vitality, life and growth; by choosing a fake plant over a real one, we symbolically choose appearance over real nourishment. Unlike other forms of decoration, such as lamps or art, which offer light or inspiration, fake plants do nothing more than pretend to be something that they're not. Over time, as the plastic plants fade and gather dust, they will become a reminder of both our inability to grow and our desire for something that we don't deserve, subconsciously affecting our motivation and optimism.

**Fix it!**

Avoid having anything fake. Ensure you only showcase an object that has a positive meaning – even if it's not alive (like art).

- Don't pressure yourself into having a plant. If you do not have a green thumb or if you travel a lot, simply skip it. It may not sound like a fix, but feng shui is all about supporting your life, not creating guilt.
- Find alternatives. What we find attractive in plants are the fresh greens that add life and colour to a home. You may substitute this feeling with art that holds vibrant blues and greens, or even by using soft furnishings like throws or cushions with the same shades.
- Borrow nature from outside. Open your windows and curtains to reveal the greenery around the home. Often, a lush green view can give the same sense of vitality without the maintenance.
- Try to have a real plant. Don't let one poor experience put you off – there are many plants that are small and hardy, so start with those. Don't overwater and remember that seeing a plant thrive can be unexpectedly rewarding.

71

# I don't like my dining table to be crowded, so it's always empty

**Rating:** 

Feng shui says... an empty table represents a home without prosperity or abundance.

**Why**

While a home that is full of clutter and mess is not good, a home that is too clean and clinical may feel empty. It is therefore important in feng shui to also add symbols of prosperity and abundance. An example is decorating your home's money corner (see page 106). Another important place that needs to signal good fortune is the dining table, as it is considered the heart of the home and should never be left empty, as that might mirror the saying, 'there is no food on the table'! A luscious bowl of fruit or vase of flowers adorning the table can signal that your home is always well fed. This idea also applies to the coffee table, which anchors the living room. In a more practical sense, a dining table that is empty or unusable due to clutter sends the message that gathering is not encouraged. Over time, this discourages connection and happy times.

**Fix it!**

Always be sure that your table looks beautiful, not empty.

- Add a bowl of fruit. This is one of the best things to place on your table, as fruit symbolises abundance and good health.
- Fresh flowers work well in the middle of your table, especially on the coffee table, as you won't necessarily eat there.
- Decorate with other types of food. Pretty crystal bowls, filled with nuts and dried fruit, or even a box of mints, can work to adorn your table without the risk of spoiling.
- Centre art or sculpture. If you are travelling and cannot have perishables at home, place a vibrant centrepiece on the table, like a colourful glass sculpture or beautiful candle holder –with candles, of course.
- Decorate the table that you actually use. If you gather round the couch, focus on the coffee table. If it's the kitchen, decorate the kitchen island.
- Use the dining table. If you don't eat there, use it for study, work or hobbies. Do not let the table be a clutter magnet or be forgotten.

# I collect beautiful vases, but I don't have enough flowers to fill them

**Rating:** 

Feng shui says... a beautiful empty vase on display means your life will be empty too.

**Why**

A vase is a vessel, and vessels are designed to contain things, be it flowers, fruit or even water. In feng shui, when you leave a vase empty, it implies that you are lacking, either because you cannot afford flowers, or that all your flowers have died because a famine has befallen you or your garden is infertile – yes, feng shui can get that dramatic. Another parallel compares a beautiful empty vase to an elegant and polished home that is devoid of love and warmth. Either way, an empty vase is a symbol of waiting for it to eventually be filled. Until then it remains a reminder of the lack in our lives.

**Fix it!**

If you have vases or vessels, use them as intended, by filling them with beautiful things.

- Put something in your vase. Add fresh flowers or any kind of pretty decoration. Avoid dead plants or flowers though, as this might make things worse.
- Rotate and refresh, especially if you have many vases. Swap them out and showcase them seasonally. Remember, any vase that acts as a table centrepiece should always be filled.
- Cap your vase with a crystal sphere or ceramic ball to signify that it's out of service.
- Reframe your vases as art by displaying them inside a glass cabinet, showing that these are decorative pieces to be admired, not for use.
- Apply the same logic to other vessels. Fruit bowls should contain fruit, and decorative plates should be placed on plate stands or hung on the wall.
- Alternative fillings to flowers and fruit would be coins or crystals, or even pebbles. The key is to signal fullness rather than emptiness.

73

# I need my phone, my tablet and my TV in my bedroom

**Rating:**

Feng shui says... having lots of electronic devices in your bedroom will disturb your mind and prevent deep rest.

**Why**

Traditionally, a bedroom is dark, quiet and still to allow for your body and mind to fully shut down. By contrast, screens and electronics introduce mental stimulation – which is why they should be kept out of the bedroom. Even when turned off, their presence reminds you of work or entertainment, keeping your mind alert. In addition, electronics often give off subtle indicators such as charging lights and humming sounds, which signal activity rather than rest, and may feel artificial and sharp.

**Fix it!**

Reduce stimulation and return the room to a more analogue state.

- Avoid having too many electronics in your room. Small things like phones and their chargers are fine (if they won't distract you).
- Turn screens and monitors away from you. These are the strongest reminders of work, especially if your desk is in your bedroom. Place computer monitors as far from you as possible – and ideally not visible from your bed.
- Create a separate sitting area for watching TV instead of watching it from the bed. If you need to watch TV to fall asleep, set a timer so it shuts itself off.
- Soften reflections. Screens act like mirrors that reflect you as you sleep, so hanging fabric to hide the screens will help you to physically tune them out, even if this makes the room look like your grandma's.
- Eliminate light noise by taping over any leaking LEDs, and do not let your flashy computer show off its fancy lights while you sleep.
- Introduce yin objects back into the room, like analogue clocks, table lamps and soft bedding.
- Generally, electronics should be treated as ancillary support to daily life, so even in non-sleeping rooms, they should be placed discreetly unless they are the central focus, like in entertainment rooms.

# I love my cute plushies, I want them all over my room

**Rating:** 

Feng shui says... figures or dolls in your bedroom create anxiety and affect outward relationships.

**Why**

Dolls and plushies may seem cute in the daytime, but at night, these figures, with their wide, never-closing eyes, stare at you in the dark as you toss yourself to sleep. Even though they are not actually alive, they still give the feeling that you are being watched, and the room won't feel restful or private. In addition, these figures share the room with you, making it difficult for you to mentally condition yourself to invite partners into your already crowded room, affecting romantic relationships. Finally, if you currently experience feelings of being judged or criticised in life or at work, the dolls might magnify these feelings, making you feel even more scrutinised.

**Fix it!**

Avoid having too many creatures in your space. This applies to anything with a face which you associate with life.

- Limit any objects with faces in your intimate areas, especially close to your bed.
- Store them in a closed box or display cabinet behind glass, especially if you have a large collection of dolls or plushies. The enclosure creates a psychological boundary – you know they won't escape at night.
- Never position them so their eyes point towards you. Eye contact makes them feel even more alive.
- There are two exceptions when it comes to having characters close to your bed. If you are single, plushies or figures can act as 'guardians' and make you feel protected. That said, limit them to just one main character, otherwise these guardians will compete with each other. The second exception is if you are partnered, and associate a pair of plushies with you and your partner, so looking at them is a reminder of your closeness. But ensure the plushies are looking at each other, and not you.

75

# I like fish, but the fish tank in my bedroom keeps me up at night

**Rating:** 

Feng shui says... having a fish tank in your bedroom will cause instability and restlessness.

### Why

Water is considered a very yang element in feng shui. It is flowing, trickling and sparkling. Adding fish, bubbles and lights turns a fish tank into a vibrant source of continuous energy. At the same time, a bedroom is meant to be still and calm to support rest. Unlike plants or electronics, which only make us *think* of energy, fish tanks are actual sources of energy in themselves, which works to keep us awake. Fish tanks represent wealth in motion, so they are best suited for higher-energy places.

### Fix it!

Keep your fish tank in a high-energy space, and keep your sleeping area calm.

- Choose the right location for your fish tank. It will work best in lively parts of your home like the living area, ideally visible from the entrance, which represents wealth flowing in. Fish tanks are also great in study rooms and offices, where you can engage with their vitality.
- Place the tank as far as possible from where you sleep, ideally at the far end of the room.
- Turn off the lights in the tank at night. Any grow lights or decorative lights should only be used during the day to match your circadian rhythm.
- Use quieter pumps and other machinery. For example, choose an internal return versus external return pump or waterfalls. The sound of moving water can keep you awake.
- Place the tank on a solid surface so it feels stable, vibrates less and is more integrated into the room.
- Always keep the tank and its contents healthy and alive. Murky water or dying fish is indeed more yin, but being dead is not the same as sleeping.
- The same principles apply to reptile tanks, bird cages and any form of animal enclosure. Always select a place that suits their energy. Pets are welcome in your bedroom, as long as they share similar sleeping hours to you.

76

# I like plants and I want to make my room feel like a rainforest

**Rating:**

Feng shui says... plants in your bedroom will prevent deep rest.

## Why

Plants are subtle creatures, so let me give a subtle analogy. Imagine being in the Stone Age, and you're looking for a place to shelter. You find a cave, but it's covered in moss and plants. You just know that it is not completely sheltered because it must be exposed to rain or sunshine for these plants to thrive. Even though we know our rooms are fully sheltered, our subconscious tells us that we might be sleeping out in the woods, making us feel slightly exposed and not entirely protected. That said, plants are not bad! They offer feelings of nurturing calm and even improve air quality during the day. It's really about putting them in the appropriate location.

## Fix it!

The key is to have the right number and types of plants in the right places.

- Keep plants away from your face and head. It's okay to have plants in the bedroom (if you must), just keep them in a nice bunch close to the window, and far from your bed.
- Choose plants that are softer in shape, or more yin. Generally, spiky plants like palms or snake plants have a lot of yang energy – they even look like the rays of the sun. Instead, go for more yin-looking plants like jade plants or succulents with roundish leaves, or plants with darker leaves that thrive in low-light conditions, like peace lilies.
- If you're after the colour and vibrance that plants give, try instead to use green- or blue-hued artwork or soft furnishings.
- If you must make your room look like a greenhouse, create a cosy, calm enclave within it. Use a canopy bed to create an enclosed, protected zone among the lushness.

77

# I want fresh flowers all over my bedroom, but my partner hates it

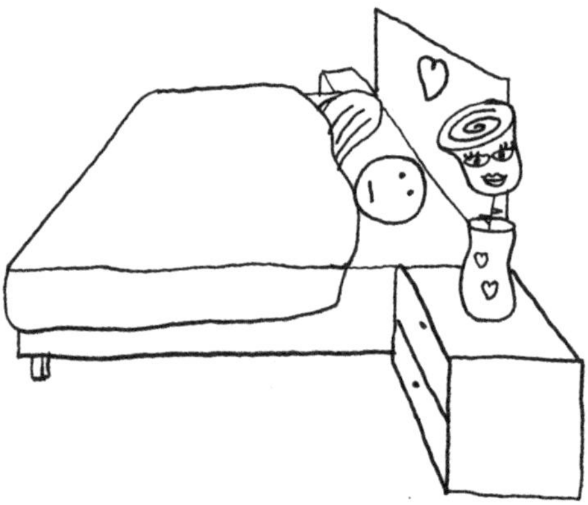

**Rating:**

Feng shui says... having fresh flowers in a couple's bedroom invites a third person into the relationship.

**Why**

Flowers are heavy with symbolism and, depending on where you put them, can carry different meanings. In the bedroom, flowers are associated with temptation and allure. When a couple shares a bedroom, it is a place for intimacy and emotional security, so this symbolism may be disruptive. That said, flowers can still work in bedrooms in specific situations; if you're recovering from illness, having flowers can bring vitality to the space. Outside of sleeping spaces, flowers should be used thoughtfully too. For example, kitchens with their strong fire energy, may not be the best place for delicate flowers, but flowering herbs could work well. In contrast, flowers work well in spaces where we want the sense of abundance that they bring.

**Fix it!**

Place the right kinds of flowers in the right kind of places. It's also important to consider the cultural symbolism of flowers. When in doubt, ask yourself what the flowers represent to you, and place them in the appropriate part of your home.

- Substitute flowers for another object if you want their vibrance but not their significance, such as textiles or artwork with floral patterns.

Below are some famous flowers and their associations to consider in your flower arranging:

- Chrysanthemums are widely associated with death and funerals in East Asian cultures.
- Lilies carry associations with mourning and their intense scent can be overwhelming.
- Roses represent passion and love. Beautiful, but maybe too romantically charged in shared spaces like living rooms.
- Tulips, being generally cheerful, are appropriate for most areas.
- Sunflowers are very high in energy and one of the rare flowers that work in a kitchen.

78

# I want a clock, can I hang it in my dining room?

**Rating:**

Feng shui says... hanging a clock prominently in your dining room means good times will come to an end.

**Why**

The dining room is seen as the heart of the home as it's where the family gathers to share meals and connection. It is an important place that represents unity and abundance. A clock, on the other hand, is a symbol of time, limits and things moving on. Its presence reminds us that this happy moment is only temporary. While a clock won't ruin relationships, it can prevent us from fully immersing ourselves in the moment and make shared times feel rushed or transactional. Clocks are better placed in rooms where the awareness of time is helpful, such as kitchens and workspaces, and avoided in places of relaxation, such as living rooms, and places that represent beginnings, such as entryways. The bedroom is interesting: while it's a place to relax, we do need to wake up, so a small and discreet alarm clock is fine.

**Fix it!**

The dining room should be decorated with objects that represent abundance and good times, not time running out.

- Avoid hanging a clock in the dining room, especially if it's clearly visible from the table.
- Put a clock in task-focused spaces like kitchens and offices.
- If a clock is placed in a living space or common area, keep it subtle and off-centre, so it's not the focus of the room.
- Avoid hanging a clock over you, for example directly over the couch or centrally over your desk, as this can feel overly intense, like you're in an examination hall.
- Choose a more calming design. For example, a clock without explicit numbers that will look more like decor, or a clock without a ticking second hand.

79

# This portrait feels very intense for my entryway, is that okay?

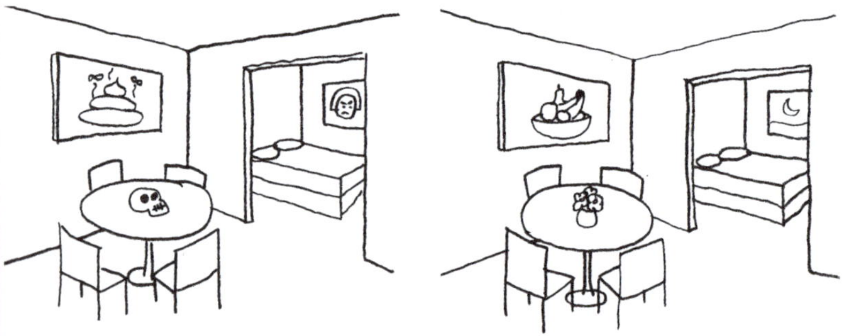

**Rating:** 

Feng shui says... a big portrait at your entrance will scare intruders away, but it can also scare you.

**Why**

The art that you hang can affect the way you feel. Portraits, especially large ones looking straight at you, can come across as strong and intimidating, almost as if the person in the picture was confronting or judging you. The art in your entry area is especially important because it makes the first impression, and sets the tone of your home. The different rooms in your home serve different emotional purposes, and choosing the wrong art can make a room feel 'off', while choosing the right art can truly enhance your space.

**Fix it!**

There are no right or wrong kinds of art. Just be aware that the type of art you hang can and will affect the way you feel.

- Entrances should feel welcoming and uplifting. Choose artwork that symbolises welcome, prosperity and abundance. In Chinese culture, fish represent abundance, but anything that you associate with your culture or feelings work.
- Living spaces can have pictures of family or artwork representing shared values, as this is where the family gathers.
- In dining spaces, show art that reminds you of abundance and harvests. Vibrant colours work particularly well to whet your appetite.
- In the bedroom, have art that is calm and relaxing, and avoid portraits of people. An exception are wedding or relationship pictures of you and your partner. But keep the photo of your mother-in-law out of your bedroom.
- Offices should have art that either motivates or represents you, especially if it can be seen in your background in virtual meetings.
- Bathrooms are fun places to hang art, because these are leftover spaces with little emotional baggage, meaning you can hang almost anything.
- But remember: you need to enjoy and feel the energy of the art that you choose, so trust your heart, and hang the pieces thoughtfully.

# COLOURS

# I am painting my front door, what colour should I choose?

**Rating:** 

Feng shui says... a wrong-colour door means missed opportunities and weak first impressions.

**Why**

In feng shui, your front door is where opportunities and fortune enter your life. Each compass direction is linked to one of the five elements, whose colours naturally resonate better with that direction. This is for the Northern Hemisphere, so reverse north and south if you are in the Southern Hemisphere.

- North (water) is the darkest side, and represented by dark blue/black.
- South (fire), as it is often in sunlight, is red or vibrant warm colours.
- East (wood) faces the rising sun, and is green to represent growth and new beginnings.
- West (metal) is where sunset happens, and is white or grey to reflect the golden hues that hit it.

It makes a big difference when you match your door with its direction, as when the colour clashes with the direction, it can feel 'off'. For example, if your door is facing the darker north side and it's painted fire red, the colour will always feel muted and dull. Or if your door faces the sunny side of the street, and it's painted a gloomy black, it will feel heavy and unwelcoming. Having the wrong door colour is a bit like if your outward appearance doesn't match your personality, and will make your home feel out of place.

**Fix it!**

Your front door should match the vibes of the direction it's facing.

- Paint your door a colour that corresponds to its direction. It does not need to be bold; even a muted version of the colour is fine.
- Use a wooden door as that is seen as a neutral grounding colour that can be used for any direction.
- Use other elements to represent your entrance's direction. If painting your door is not an option, reinforce the energy with decor: for north, use water elements; for south, use vibrant flowers; for east, use plants and vines; and for west, use metal objects and round shapes.

81

# My kitchen is all black and it looks nice, but I have no appetite to cook

**Rating:**

Feng shui says... an all-black kitchen means suppressed nourishment and weakened vitality.

**Why**

In feng shui, the kitchen represents the fire element. It is a place of nourishment, abundance and warmth. On the other hand, black – being cool and dark – represents the water element. If your kitchen is a glossy black, the fire energy may be suppressed. To help understand this, picture life in the old days, where you are a farmer. The kitchen is where bountiful harvests are brought into the home to be turned into nourishing meals. Now imagine your kitchen is damp and dark. The harvests feel vulnerable, the energy of the space is dampened, and even the food will feel less appetising.

**Fix it!**

Try to make your kitchen feel warm and inviting, regardless of its material.

- Avoid the wrong colour. There is actually no 'right' colour, but stay away from too much of the water element, which are dark blues or blacks. If you want colour, go for more muted tones so there is no excess of a certain element. Think sage green instead of emerald, or terracotta instead of bright red. Still the same tones, just calmer.

- Choose the right materials. Because a kitchen is a tactile place, natural materials work best. Wood, stone and fired tiles are great earthy materials. This doesn't mean you can't have a clean, minimalist look, as long as you choose lighter, warmer materials over glossy dark ones.

- Add vibrant elements to counter the cold feeling of a dark kitchen. If your kitchen is already black, choose decor with vibrant hues; artwork and plants will also add life and bring balance to your space.

- Use the right lighting. Warm, indirect lighting will make the kitchen feel cosy and inviting, counteracting the coldness of the dark surfaces.

82

# I’m afraid of colour, so my room is all neutral and beige

**Rating:**

Feng shui says... a fully beige room will drain your energy and inspiration.

### Why

In feng shui, a successful room contains a mix of all five elements: wood, fire, metal, water and earth. Neutral and beige sit firmly within the earth element. While an earthy, neutral room might feel calm and grounding with its wooden floors, beige walls and cream curtains, having nothing else might make it feel too lifeless, like being in a desert. This is why the other elements are needed – to ensure the balance of energy. The use of these elements is not tied to compass directions, but to specific materials and textures.

### Fix it!

Introduce all five elements into the room to various degrees.

- Earth as the base. In most homes, this is already present in the form of wooden flooring and furniture, along with creamy walls and curtains.
- Wood to add life. Not to be confused with actual wood, in feng shui wood refers to freshness and life, which you might associate with plants. Add lively plants and decor with botanicals, greens and light blues to liven up the space.
- Water to add depth. Not any blue, but very dark blues or even black. Don't overdo it; add black in the form of thin picture frames or lighting fixtures for crisp contrast.
- Metal to lift and add clarity. Represented by the colours white and grey, as well as circular shapes. Round mirrors work well, or choose furniture with a metallic element.
- Fire to add energy. This can come in the form of vibrant tones through artwork, fresh flowers or interesting light fixtures. These are small but powerful fixes that add spice and energy to your space.
- You don't need equal amounts of each element; the proportions will naturally change depending on the room's energy.

83

# My room is bright and sunny, but I want to paint it black

**Rating:**

Feng shui says... painting your room in a colour opposing its natural energy will cause energy clashes and wasted efforts.

### Why

In feng shui, the direction that your room's windows face gives it a certain energy. You should match that energy to your room's overall feel. While each direction has a set of colours associated with it (see page 189 for colours and their directions), it is not as simple as painting the walls a colour that goes with its element. Creating a room that works with its direction is about incorporating elements that bring about that energy. Instead of simply painting a south-facing room red, think instead of the feel: a south-facing room is vibrant and energetic. To balance inside and out, introduce more fire elements to align the energy. So a dark colour isn't forbidden for your sunny room – but the colour needs to be balanced with enough light and warmth to prevent the room from feeling suppressed.

### Fix it!

Align your room's aesthetics with its natural energy and feel.

- North-facing rooms are softer, cooler and more calming. Think deeper colours, heavier textiles.
- South-facing rooms are bright and vibrant, with lots of flowers, lively artwork and fiery tones.
- East-facing rooms are fresh and uplifting, with lots of plants, and fresh blues and greens.
- West-facing rooms are bright but calm, light and glossy but not too colourful.
- Don't only go by direction. Sometimes in a south-facing room the sun might be blocked, which puts the room in shadow and can make it feel more like a north-facing room energetically.
- Trust your instincts. Overall, this part is about aesthetics. The key is to love how your room looks, and don't be afraid of trying colours/ decoration out.

STORAGE

AND

CLUTTER

# My home is full of clutter and I have no room for storage

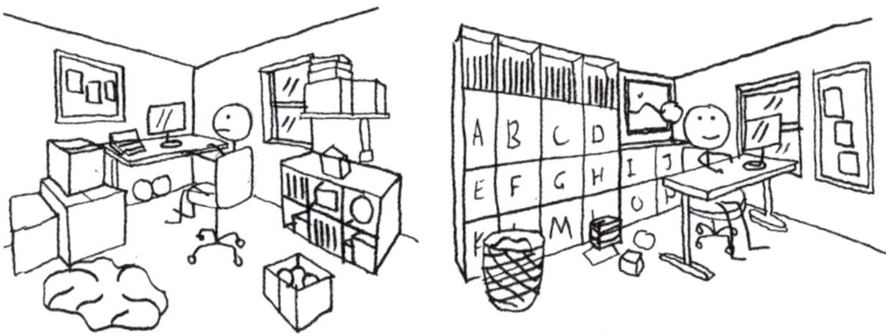


**Rating:**

Feng shui says... a cluttered home blocks opportunities and prevents growth and fresh energy from entering your life.

**Why**

Feng shui does not actually address clutter, because clutter is a relative term. What may appear as clutter to one person might be precious keepsakes or useful tools to another. What we want to avoid is when things become so disorganised that it creates stress. Then it becomes difficult to keep track of what you have and where things are, which can make you feel unsettled and overwhelmed. So, apart from the obvious fact that a messy home is bad to look at, it can weigh heavily on our psychology and emotions.

**Fix it!**

Here is a three-pronged approach to dealing with clutter and ensuring it stays organised.

- Have enough storage. This is the most obvious solution! This can be challenging (if you don't have built-in storage), but it's very important. However, it won't be that impactful unless you do the things below.
- Have a proper system for storing things. Having enough storage is only one part of solving clutter: you need to create a categorised system that allows your things to be easily found and easily stored. This will reduce resistance and uncertainty. For example, keeping all your clothes in your bedroom, cleaning supplies in the utility closet, books in the study – and don't let the categories mix.
- Understand your habits and tendencies. This is the most powerful step. When you work with your natural habits, tidying will occur naturally. For example, if you have ADHD, your mind may naturally jump between tasks. Instead of fighting this, adjust your home's systems and layout to support the way you function. Bringing related activities closer together can help turn distractions into something constructive, maximising productivity.

85

# I leave my trash in my entryway, it's just temporary I promise

**Rating:**

Feng shui says... bags of recycling, rubbish or clutter in your entryway will block fortune from coming into your home.

### Why

Your entryway is the mouth of your home, where energy, wealth and opportunities enter. Cluttering it signals that you do not welcome these into your life. Symbolism aside, being greeted by a mountain of clutter every time you return creates a poor first impression. This doesn't just apply to guests – the most important person to impress is yourself. Even though you know your own home, the entrance is where you subconsciously compare what you've seen in the outside world with your own space and your own life. If this entry moment creates dissatisfaction, disappointment or even dread, over time this can drain your motivation and make you feel disconnected from your home.

### Fix it!

First impressions count, so make your entryway feel welcoming and beautiful.

- Keep it clear. Never place trash or recycling in the entryway or within sight of the door. If possible, store the bags in a utility room or boot room. If you don't have such spaces, don't take the bags out until you are ready.
- Curate the journey into your home. Shoes, coats and daily-use items are fine, but keep them stored, ideally in blind spots not immediately noticeable from the entrance, like behind the door or inside cupboards.
- Make your entrance beautiful. Decorate it with vibrant artwork or plants, which represent abundance or prosperity. This may sound unnecessary, but such objects tell you that your home and life are in a good place.
- Ensure an effortless entry. Your door should be able to open fully, and the path into your house should be smooth and obstacle-free.
- If you must keep your trash close to the entrance, add a nice-looking bin with a lid that can always be closed.

86

# I store all my shoes nicely on a tall rack, but it still feels wrong

**Rating:**

Feng shui says... shoes stacked high up in your entryway will make you feel submissive and suppressed.

**Why**

Shoes are associated with the dirty outside world, and placing them at eye level or, even worse, above head height, can make you feel like you are being stepped on. This does not only apply to shoes, but other things that belong to the ground, such as bicycles, shovels, brooms and mops. In many Asian cultures, including China, kneeling is associated with showing respect to an elder or senior figure. Storing shoes higher than you can create a subconscious sense of inferiority or pressure from above every time you or a guest enters your home. Practically, dust and dirt may literally fall over you, which is not a nice feeling.

**Fix it!**

Things that belong to the ground should be stored below you, physically and metaphorically.

- Anything that belongs to the ground should be stored below waist level, so shoe benches are fine.
- Brooms, mops and shovels should never be displayed in the open, as they represent dirt and cleaning, symbolically 'sweeping' away any good fortune entering the home.
- Use closed cabinets. If you need to store shoes higher up, keep them hidden from view. Even so, within the shelves, store cleaner, more refined pairs above and muddy boots below.
- Point the shoes inwards so they are 'walking' into the house rather than kicking you out.
- Bicycles are better on the floor than hung high up. Ideally, never suspend a bicycle over the hallway where people walk. If you need to use a wall mount, keep the wheels below shoulder height.

87

# The living room is nice and airy, so I hang my laundry there to dry

**Rating:**

Feng shui says... hanging your laundry in the open will cause your private matters to be exposed publicly.

**Why**

Laundry racks full of underwear and crumpled clothes not only look bad, but are also akin to airing private matters in public. Clothes represent both our outward identity and our most intimate inner selves. Displaying them in the open can invite guests to see and speculate who we are, while also revealing that we are incomplete and scattered – think of those mismatched socks. Even if you don't have guests over regularly, laundry on display reminds us of unfinished work, which can subtly make us feel unsettled, or even guilty.

**Fix it!**

It's all about choosing the right place and right way to hang our laundry.

- Avoid the main living spaces. Resist hanging laundry in your living room, entry foyer or any area visible from the front door.
- Avoid spaces where you spend a lot of time. If you work from home, keep laundry out of the home office or any other place that you spend time in.
- Use your utility room. If you have a laundry room, utility space or drying yard, hang laundry there.
- Choose less-used parts of the home, such as guest rooms or even your own bedroom, since you only go in at night.
- If you hang your clothes on your balcony, place the rack where it's not easily seen from the main room.
- If your living room happens to receive the best sunlight and you really want to dry your clothes there, keep them in a blind spot, like behind the door, or along a wall outside of your main line of sight. Keep racks low and avoid overhead hangers.

88

# Clothes are scattered all over my room, it's so messy

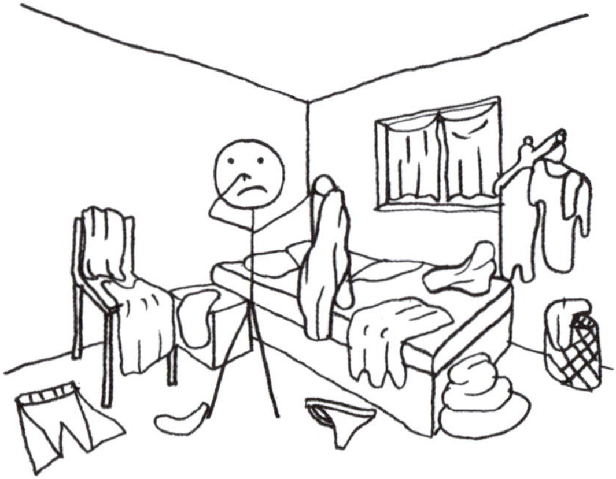

**Rating:** 

Feng shui says... piles of clothes around your room can weaken your energy and identity.

**Why**

In feng shui, clutter hinders the good flow of energy. Clothes strewn around your bedroom is a prime example of this and can feel overwhelming. Clothes also carry an additional symbolic weight: they form our outward appearance. Leaving them scattered shamefully around is like letting your self-image dissolve into a pile of lumpy fabric, suggesting that the energy you so carefully build for the world to see is nothing more than a transient mask. This is why it is important to always hang your clothes or place them nicely, as a reflection of yourself. This applies especially to those clothes that have been worn once, so they are too clean for laundry, yet too dirty to go back into the closet.

**Fix it!**

Clothes should always be placed in a tidy, respectful manner.

- Create an area for half-used clothes. Depending on how often you get changed, this could be a small corner or a large rack. Hang or fold these immediately after taking them off to avoid crumpling. If you do not have space for a rack, leave them neatly folded on a chair.
- Designate a laundry area and have a convenient basket for dirty clothes. While having a lid on the basket can make it look tidier, if it stops you from using it, it's better to not have one.
- Work with your habits. Create a clothes-storage system that you can maintain. If you dislike folding clothes, hang them up instead by having a long clothing rack with multiple hangers or by allocating storage bins so you can dump items in, which works well for underwear and socks.
- Do a daily sweep. Spend five minutes every morning or night returning your clothes to their designated areas, as this will prevent the piles from getting out of control.

# I have no storage, so I put everything under my bed

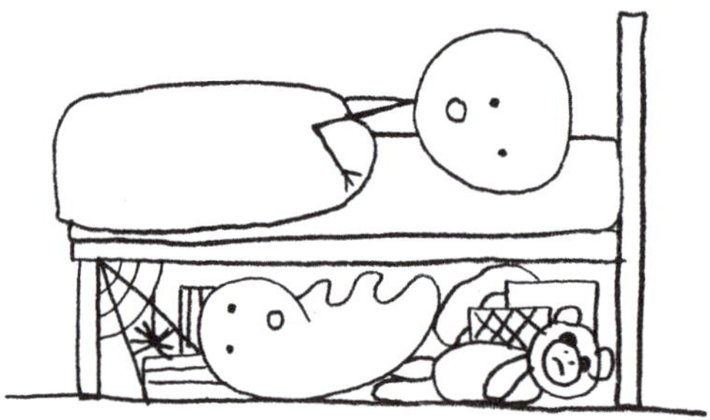

**Rating:**

Feng shui says... storing lots of things under the bed can restrict the flow of energy, affecting sleep and health.

**Why**

Sleeping is a restorative process; a time where the heavy energy of the day dissipates and we wake up recharged and rejuvenated. When your bed is crowded with things underneath, it restricts the movement of energy. Not only that, it psychologically makes you feel like the clutter and worries of life are always lingering below you. Metaphors aside, when we sleep, our bodies give off heat and moisture which needs air to circulate. When the bed is stuffed full of things, it can trap moisture and create a musty environment below. That said, if storage is limited, it is still better to store things under your bed than allow clutter to collect around you.

**Fix it!**

It's fine to store things under the bed as long as you are selective and organised.

- Leave space for air to circulate. Even if there are things under your bed, ensure that it's not too packed and that air can still circulate, so the heat and moisture can dissipate.
- Choose storage beds. Loose boxes or baskets can feel messy and chaotic, and you risk things disappearing under your bed. Instead, get purpose-made beds with built-in drawers, or lift-up beds so you can keep your things organised.
- Be selective of what goes under the bed. Choose calming, sleep-related items like bedding and linens. Out-of-season clothes or other textiles are fine too. Avoid storing items which have heavy emotional or intellectual weight, such as books or memories, as these may make your sleeping environment feel mentally or emotionally heavy.

90

# I need extra storage and the only space is over my bed

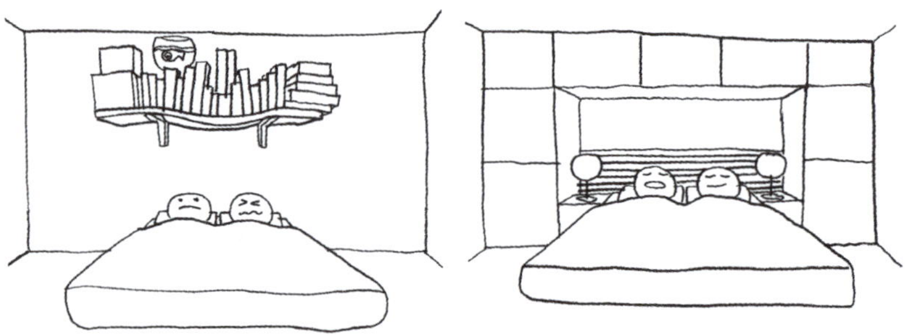

**Rating:** 

Feng shui says... a big cupboard or shelf over your bed will cause headaches and restless nights.

**Why**

While you won't actually get a headache from a big cupboard over your head, a large object looming precariously over your face while you are in your most vulnerable state can feel unsettling, especially if it is filled with heavy things. Even if everything was installed securely, your mind can wander to the worst-case scenarios: an earthquake, or the wall giving way. Such thoughts, minor as they may seem, can cast a shadow of doubt, creating tension and worry as you try to sleep. Over time, this can affect your ability to fully rest, and may contribute to poorer sleep.

**Fix it!**

Try not to have heavy things above you as you sleep, or make them feel as light as possible.

- Avoid storage or shelves above the bed. If the space above your bed feels too empty, consider a lightweight piece of art, like a tapestry. The second-best option is pictures, but hang them securely rather than placing them on shelves. If you really want open shelves, have only a single, thin shelf for light decorative items – no plants and definitely don't have books.

- Reduce visual heaviness. Choose closed cupboards over open shelves so the items are less obvious, and paint the cupboards the same colour as the walls so they blend in.

- Create a sense of support. Add sturdy-looking brackets under the shelves or combine the overhead cupboards with tall wardrobes on either side so the cupboard is a visual 'bridge' over your bed instead of just floating. This will give a visual assurance that the units above you are well supported.

- Lift the energy upward. Use a headboard with LED strips to 'push' the energy up and make the shelves look less heavy. Table lamps on either side can achieve a similar effect.

- The above guidelines also apply to storage over your sofa, so hang artwork instead.

91

# There's a shelf full of books over my desk, I hope they don't fall on me

**Rating:**

Feng shui says... if you have a shelf full of things above you when you work, you will suffer from pressure and lack of clarity.

**Why**

A big shelf above your desk may seem like a space-saving solution, but it can cause unnecessary mental pressure. Unlike typical overhead storage, a shelf located over a workspace is usually 'active' storage accessed throughout the day, such as for files and stationery. These items represent your workload and tasks looming over you, and are symbolic of work piling up and overwhelming you, adding to the pressure. Metaphors aside, these shelves cast shadows, making your workspace feel darker. Such feelings of mental weight and overshadowing will only add to the stress of work. Kitchen storage is different, as you are standing and moving, so shelves over a kitchen counter feel less heavy.

**Fix it!**

With any overhead storage, try to make it feel less heavy by minimising or curating it.

- Reduce overhead storage where possible. Store things low, under your desk or in cupboards.
- Keep shelves shallow. Ideally shelves should not project more than a foot or 30cm, so they feel like they are in front of you and not above.
- Be selective of what goes on these shelves. Avoid heavy files and paperwork and, if possible, no work-related things at all.
- Choose light and uplifting items for exposed shelves. Awards and certificates work well above a desk as they symbolise aspiration rather than pressure. Similarly, exposed kitchen shelves are best used for displaying your most-loved (but not cracked!) plates or glassware (see page 152).
- Use closed storage when you need to actually store supplies, and paint the storage doors to blend in with the walls, so they visually recede.
- Add lighting. For utilitarian spaces, add LED strips under the shelves to illuminate your workspace, rather than cast a shadow over it.

# OUTSIDE

# THE

# HOME

92

# My window faces a cemetery, it gives me goosebumps

**Rating:** 

Feng shui says... if your window faces a cemetery, your soul will be sucked away.

### Why

A cemetery contains hundreds of dead people; this constantly reminds us of death. More importantly, a cemetery is a very yin place, with not much vitality, the direct opposite of yang, or life. Having your home close to such a yin place may make you feel as if you are the only life form around, causing you to feel isolated, detached and lifeless yourself. Over time, these feelings of heaviness and melancholy will affect your inner energy and personality. Not all cemeteries are the same though. An old cemetery which has been turned into a park with lots of greenery is much better as a neighbour than an active cemetery. The size of the cemetery also matters. If it's small and surrounded by other houses, the yin energy is countered by all the lively homes around.

### Fix it!

There are two main ways to deal with cemeteries: either hide them from view, or counter them with yang energy.

- Limit exposure. Choose homes where only a few windows face towards the cemetery, ideally from the kitchen or bathroom.
- Block the view. If you have a large number of windows facing the cemetery, use curtains or blinds to cover them.
- 'Fortify' the windows by hanging lively, sparkly crystals to absorb the energy or, as a last resort, a bagua mirror facing out.
- Do not use wind chimes. Even though they represent yang energy, they are said to attract wandering spirits.
- Add vibrant, lively energy to your home through art and colour choices, and by having lots of plants, especially ones that represent life, like bamboo, close to the windows.
- Add warmth in the form of lights in the home, which symbolise life, and keep your spaces dry and fragrant with warming scents.

93

# My home is next to a big hospital and the sirens make me sad

**Rating:** 

Feng shui says... if you live too close to a hospital, you will easily get sick.

**Why**

Hospitals are associated with illness, pain and loss. Unlike a cemetery, which is still and passive, hospitals are charged with active emotions of urgency and suffering. Seeing and hearing ambulances come and go, and lights burning through the night, can be a constant reminder of this vulnerability. Such feelings not only drain you, but also create feelings of guilt and fear. Guilt in seeing others in great pain, and fear that illnesses are uncomfortably close. Over time, you might feel anxious and vulnerable with the hospital absorbing all the positive energy around the neighbourhood. That said, not all hospitals carry the same energy. Maternity wards, rehabilitation centres and wellness-focused facilities are associated with life and hope, so the impact does depend on which part of the hospital your home faces.

**Fix it!**

The idea is to focus on the positive sides of the hospital and reduce emotional exposure.

- Understand what you are actually facing. Hospitals are large and complex and there is a good chance you are simply facing administrative facilities. The only parts you really want to avoid are views of the emergency areas, ambulance bays or morgues.
- Reduce visual reminders by blocking the view of the hospital from inside your home. Hang blinds or curtains to soften the view. You may even hang colourful crystals to absorb the energy if you don't want to add curtains.
- Avoid hostile cures. Do not use a bagua mirror, for example, as this is a hostile gesture towards a place of care and help.
- Add a water feature like a fountain to mask the distant sounds of sirens and mechanical noise.
- Strengthen your home's energy by having warm lights and vibrant artwork.

94

# My neighbour is mean, should I move out?

**Rating:** 

Feng shui says... bad neighbours give out negative energy and will cause you stress and emotional drain.

### Why

Neighbours are not a traditional part of feng shui, but environmental energy is. Even though you don't actually live with your neighbours, they are close enough to affect your sense of calm and mental wellbeing. This not only applies to extreme situations like antisocial behaviour; sometimes subtle signals can have a strong impact. Cold stares, passive aggressiveness or general hostility can affect your ability to relax, and could even fuel negative feelings towards your home. The same principle applies to disruptive commercial neighbours, construction sites, even abandoned homes. If you are constantly on the edge, your home will no longer feel like home.

### Fix it!

There are several feng shui defences, but ultimately it depends on the type of negative energy that your neighbours give.

- Try to talk to them. Be kind and reasonable and always have empathy. This is the hardest solution, but also the most effective, as it has the potential to turn negative energy into positive.
- Block them out. Use plants, hedges or screens to prevent direct views of their property. This will help you not to think about them, particularly if your neighbours are noisy commercial sites that you have no control over. If you live in an apartment, add plants or wind chimes in the hallway.
- Create positive vibes in your home – that will help you to not think about them. It is your home, after all, and your neighbours are blocked once the door is shut. Add plants, pretty artwork and warm lighting to your space. If you can focus on the positives in your life, the negatives outside are more easily forgotten. This works well for haunted houses next door too.
- Use sound intentionally. Add fountains to create soothing sounds to drown out any noises, or use music.
- Add guardians to your door, such as a pair of fu dogs or lions. These help to give a sense of protection and reminds your neighbours that you exist, so they might be more respectful.

# My house is right at the end of a T-junction, is it bad?

**Rating:** 

Feng shui says... when a road points at your house, you will be bombarded with constant attacks and misfortune.

**Why**

In feng shui, a road is a very strong source of energy, and when it points straight at your home, whether you're at a T-junction, the corner of a road or in the middle of a cul-de-sac, it is called a poison arrow due to its aggressive force. Here, your home is very exposed to anyone driving down the road and, in rare cases, cars that lose control might crash right into your front gate! More importantly, whenever you look out the windows the sight of a long straight road pointing towards you can cause unease and tension. Note that the longer the road, the more energy it inflicts. This principle also applies to landscaping, albeit less intensely. If you have a pathway leading to your door, a winding path feels better than a long, straight one.

**Fix it!**

Protect your home from the bombardment of energy as much as possible.

- Add a barrier, like a wall, fence or hedge. The more it hides your house, the better. It does not need to be high, as long as it blocks the view of the cars and creates a sense of calm between you and the road.
- Shield the windows. Use curtains or blinds to block the view of the oncoming road and its traffic. You can use cafe curtains or frost the bottom half of the windows, so that you don't see the cars but still get the light. Or hang crystals inside the road-facing windows. This will provide a psychological barrier and help distract you and soften the energy.
- Divert the energy. If possible, add a roundabout or build a fountain in front of your house, or shift the entry gate of your home to the left or right of your plot to redirect the flow.
- Calm the energy. Instead of a driveway, landscape the front of your home into a beautiful and calming garden. This helps to soften the energy coming from the road before it reaches your home. In your garden, use windy paths rather than straight ones to avoid mimicking the road.
- Add guardians in front of your door to protect your home, for example a pair of fu dogs or stone lions.

96

# The road in front is higher than my house, I feel like a hobbit

**Rating:**

Feng shui says... if your home is lower than the ground around you, bad fortune will accumulate and you will face constant struggles.

### Why

It is said that your house should never sit lower than the ground around it, and there is a very practical reason for this: if there is a flood, your house would be the first to be submerged. Of course, these days, modern drainage systems reduce this risk, but being lower than the street still has its challenges. A road is seen as a river in feng shui, and all its rushing and aggressive energy will pour downwards to you, both metaphorically and physically. Being 'lower' than everyone else will also make you feel like you are constantly being overlooked by people passing, plus the pollution and dust from moving cars will settle on your doorstep. Over time, you will feel overshadowed, pressed down, or even bullied by your surroundings.

### Fix it!

You need to make your home feel elevated, protected and confident.

- Prioritise the front door. Even if your home is largely underground, ensure that the front door itself isn't overshadowed.
- Create an open forecourt. Build a low retaining wall or terrace the area immediately in front of your door to create an open and level forecourt that is open to the sky.
- Use hedges and plants. Hide the higher ground with hedges and tall greenery so it looks like a garden, rather than just earth.
- Elevate your door. Lift your door up from the landing so you always 'step up' into your home.
- Enhance your entry. Adorn it with door guardians, lights and vibrant colours to give it presence and confidence.
- Control interior views. Use bottom-up blinds or cafe curtains to manage the views from inside the house, so that you see the sky and not the road.
- Focus on the backyard. If the land in front of your house slopes up, it usually means your backyard is sloping down, so focus your views and energy there.

97

# There is a big tree in front of my house, it blocks my view

**Rating:**

Feng shui says... a big tree right in front of your house will block opportunities and stand in the way of success.

**Why**

Imagine you are driving on a single-lane road, and ahead of you is a huge truck moving slowly. You can't see beyond it, and because it's a single lane, you can't overtake it either. So you are stuck trailing it for miles. Frustrating, right? Having a big tree in front of your house gives a similar feeling, where the sense of openness and views are blocked. In feng shui, we say that the tree blocks good energy from reaching your home, along with all the fortune and opportunities that it might bring. Practically, a tall tree blocks views and light from your front door and windows, overshadowing your home and making it feel dark and heavy, almost shutting you away from the outside world. This applies to any tall, imposing objects nearby, like street-lamps, pylons or traffic lights. Even a thin street-lamp can affect you. Picture this: you have a lovely sea-view apartment, and there is a lamp-post right in front of you. It does not really block the view, but ruins the openness.

**Fix it!**

If you cannot get rid of the obstruction, the best way is to redirect your focus.

- Consider the obstruction. Next time you are shopping for a home, be aware of the openness in front of the house and avoid those with tall trees or other objects right in front.
- Side placement is fine. Trees around your home can be wonderful, so, to be specific, you just want the tree to not block your front door.
- Redirect movement. Build or change your pathway and landscaping to flow around the tree, so it appears as though the tree is standing to the side rather than in front.
- Trim the tree (if it's yours). Thinning the branches or removing dense foliage can reduce the heaviness, just like how trees in winter feel more open.
- Rearrange the furniture inside. If you live in an apartment and your view is blocked from your sofa, rearrange your internal layout so that you at least have a partial view from where you are seated.

# I want a fountain in my backyard, where should it go?

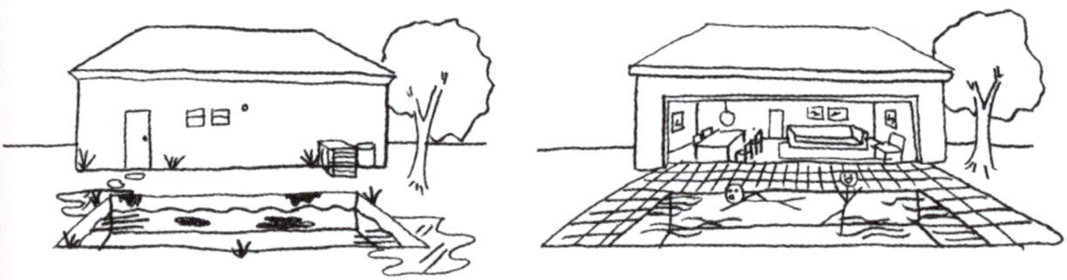

**Rating:** 

Feng shui says... a fountain or water feature in the wrong place can erode your prosperity.

**Why**

Water, with its association with rivers and seas, trade and produce, is generally seen as a symbol of wealth and abundance. However, water also has the power to flood and destroy. This is why in feng shui water features should be placed in front of the house and not behind, so you can observe and benefit from them. The more tangible reason is that in traditional houses, the front is where energy, people and opportunities enter, while the back is more passive and hidden from view. That said, modern houses often place their main social spaces towards the back, so this rule should be adapted to suit your home's layout, as you might wish to enjoy viewing a water feature from your sofa.

**Fix it!**

Choose a location so the fountain is prominent and can be enjoyed.

- Place it in front of the house. This is the traditional advice: with water flowing towards the home rather than away, it symbolises wealth arriving instead of leaving.
- Water can be behind the home, as long as the main living space faces the back. If your house is designed so that your family room opens generously towards the backyard, then this placement is acceptable.
- Avoid water features being seen by nobody. If your home is designed with only the laundry room, bathrooms and kitchen facing the back, it is better not to have a water feature there.
- If you want a pool and the backyard is the only option, but no living space faces it, place the pool to one side, or further from the house.
- Always ensure your water feature is clean and flowing. Never allow it to stagnate or run dry, as poorly maintained water is considered inauspicious. If you cannot maintain it, it's better not to have it at all.

# GENERAL

99

# Do pets need good feng shui too?

**Rating:**

Feng shui says... if your pets have bad feng shui, they will suffer and you will suffer along with them.

### Why

Pets are seen as the guardians of your energy. They breathe life into your home and support your need to nurture, while offering protection and love in return. When they don't feel safe and happy, your own emotions might mirror theirs; perhaps you might feel tense and agitated, or even worry and feel guilt when they are unwell. Animals and humans both feel and experience their environment, so it is important to ensure that your pets feel protected and calm. So yes, feng shui-ing your pets' spaces is important.

### Fix it!

Understand your pets' natural habitats and needs, and create an environment that they like. These are general guidelines and I recommend you do further reading to understand your pets' needs, so you can create a happy home for them.

- For free-roaming animals like cats, dogs and rabbits, ensure they have safe places to relax that are not in main pathways, and that their toilet areas are far from their safe spaces. Also create spots for them to hang out with good views.
- For caged animals like rats, hamsters, chinchillas and the like, ensure their cages are not in high-traffic areas. Within their cages, they should have safe zones to rest out of sight, and higher activity areas where they can eat, poop and clean.
- For birds, ensure they get lots of good views around the room and receive a natural, indirect light.
- For reptiles, ensure their cages have the right temperature and lighting control, and that the environment looks pleasant, with lots of plants and natural rocks with spaces to hide and bask.
- For fish and other aquarium animals, ensure the water is always clean and running, and that the tank itself looks nice with plants and decor. In feng shui, water and fish are associated with wealth.

100

# Oh no! My home is breaking every single feng shui rule

Feng shui says... if you don't follow feng shui, your life will be ruined.

**Why**

Scared? Don't be. Let me explain. The path your life takes, whether you are healthy, happy or wealthy, depends on three things:

- Luck (heaven): Being born into a rich family, surviving an earthquake, or winning the lottery. These are things that can affect your life, but are completely out of your control.
- Personality (you): Your passion, your dedication, the work you put in, these are entirely within your control and shape where you go in life.
- Environment (earth): This is what most people forget. The spaces you live in, sleep in and spend your time in influence how supported, energised and focused you feel. From obvious things like how peaceful your bedroom is, or how inspiring your study feels, to small things, like the kind of decorations you use that might motivate you, or even the best nails to keep your pictures safely on the wall during that earthquake. Feng shui is about giving you the right environment so you can be your best.

**Fix it!**

If your home is full of feng shui faux pas, don't panic. You don't need perfection; just focus on what matters most.

- Be far from bad energy. Avoid being in the middle of circulation paths, or being surrounded by stressful things.
- Be close to good energy. Be close to natural light, views, pretty plants, and keep your spaces happy and uplifting.
- Focus on where you spend the most time. We cannot make our homes perfect, but the places where you spend the most time should consistently feel nice.
- Always feel positive. Finally, feng shui is all about feeling comfortable and supported. Everyone is different, so listen to yourself, trust your feelings and, however it may look, make your home feel like home to you: always safe, always welcoming, always joyful!

# Conclusion

So there you have it! You are now armed with an abundance of knowledge of the most common feng shui rules and what they actually mean for you, and it's not as scary as it sounds, right?

Not only that, you now know how to fix these little problems, so go through your home, look around, and see what bugs you. Start with the issues that bother you the most, and fix them one by one. Slowly but surely, you will build a nicer, happier home for yourself which, hopefully, will reflect in your psyche, translating into a more confident, positive and abundant life.

And the best part? This priceless knowledge is something that once you know, you can't unknow, and it will stay with you forever.

So... now you know!

# About the author

Cliff Tan is an author, architect, space planner and feng shui practitioner. He is known as Dear Modern on social media where he teaches about space planning and feng shui and has amassed millions of followers on TikTok, Instagram and YouTube. His first book, *Feng Shui Modern*, was a bestseller, and he plans to continue educating and sharing his knowledge. Cliff is from Singapore and based in London.

# Acknowledgements

I would like to thank everyone who has shown interest and support in my knowledge and content, inspiring me to do what I do. My partner, Béla, who taught me to stop whining about a problem and, rather, to fix it! And Lauren, my dear editor, who first discovered me, and believed in this second book.

# Index by room

Entryway



Bathroom



Living room



Dining room

First published in the United Kingdom
in 2026 by
Batsford
43 Great Ormond Street
London
WC1N 3HZ

An imprint of B. T. Batsford Holdings Limited





Commissioning editor: Lauren Whybrow
Designer and typesetter: Christopher O'Leary
Line illustrations: Cliff Tan
Internal and cover gradients: Hoi Chan
Proofreaders: Kate Quarry and Kitty Stogdon

ISBN 9781837330744

A CIP catalogue record for this book is available from the British Library.

10 9 8 7 6 5 4 3 2 1

Reproduction by Rival Colour Ltd, UK
Printed by Toppan Leefung Printing International Ltd, China

This book can be ordered direct from the publisher at www.batsfordbooks.com, or try your local bookshop

Distributed throughout the UK and Europe by Abrams & Chronicle Books, 1st Floor, 22–24 Ely Place, London EC1N 6TE and 57 rue Gaston Tessier, 75166 Paris, France

www.abramsandchronicle.co.uk | info@abramsandchronicle.co.uk